Cultures of Exile

Polygons: Cultural Diversities and Intersections
General Editor: **Lieve Spaas**, *Professor of French Cultural Studies, Kingston University, UK*

CULTURES OF EXILE

Images of Displacement

Edited by Wendy Everett and
Peter Wagstaff

Berghahn Books
NEW YORK · OXFORD

First published in 2004 by

Berghahn Books
www.BerghahnBooks.com

Library of Congress Cataloging-in-Publication Data

Cultures of exile : images of displacement / edited by
Wendy Everett and Peter Wagstaff.
    p. cm.-- (Polygons; v. 7)
Includes bibliographical references and index.
ISBN 1-57181-591-0 (alk. paper)
    1. Marginality, Social. 2. Marginality, Social, in motion
pictures. 3. Exiles. 4. Emigration and immigration.
5. Migration, Internal. I. Everett, Wendy E. (Wendy Ellen),
1945- II. Wagstaff, Peter. III. Series.

HM1136.C85 2003
305.5'68–dc22   2003057827

British Library Cataloguing in Publication Data

A catalogue record for this book is available
from the British Library.

ISBN 1-57181-591-0 (hardback)
Printed in United Kingdom by Biddles / IBT Global

CONTENTS

PART III   BODY

≋ ≋

LIST OF ILLUSTRATIONS

≈ ≈

INTRODUCTION

As the turbulent, terrifying and exhilarating twentieth century drew to its close, to be replaced by the even more terrifying beginnings of a new millennium, it has been particularly fascinating to observe the extent to which long-standing historical, political, and geographical experiences of exile came to assume a significance which both included and transcended their specific circumstances. Given that exile must now be recognised as a key concept affecting virtually every aspect of contemporary life, there could be no more fitting moment for the publication of this volume of essays, whose multiple perspectives and wide-ranging analyses explore and develop the simple proposition that the experience of exile constitutes the major defining experience of the modern world.

While narratives of exile are a cultural commonplace, deeply rooted in human consciousness and offering a founding myth that is readily translated into the everyday experiences of populations and generations, it is perhaps the coming together of the political and the economic on a hitherto unimaginable scale that has marked the last hundred years as the century of the migrant and the exile. Importantly, while the Irish, the Italian, and the Middle-European diasporas were crossing the Atlantic, other equally transforming if less spectacular journeys were also taking place. The inexorable spread of mechanisation and industrialisation, for example, caused whole generations to desert the stable if penurious existence of the peasant for the precarious world of the urban proletariat, and it is clear that the atomised culture of life in the city is a central factor in the sense of estrangement and alienation that characterises much twentieth-century thought and artistic creativity. Thus exile within the home, within the family becomes as potent a form of alienation and despair as its more spectacular corollaries. In all this, the unifying thread is the impact on individual human lives of a movement away from a fixed and trusted centre and into a fractured and disorientating world. Actual experience and myth come together in the realisation that the movement away from home is both a spatial and a temporal dislocation; that the unknown land beyond the borders of a previously secure existence is also an unknown and unforeseeable future.

It is not enough, therefore, to think of exile exclusively in terms of the spatial and temporal estrangement of individuals forced to abandon their place – and time – of origin. So pervasive is the trope of exile that it has come to be seen as a potent metaphor for a range of phenomena concerned with the distinctive, the disjunctive and the alienated. Just as the exiled individual may be robbed of birthright and cultural inheritance, so too she or he may be robbed of selfhood, of the holistic conjunction of mind, spirit and body, through violation or exploitation. The same sense of exile, or alienation, may result for the individual who is marginalised, cast adrift, by the inability or unwillingness to conform to the tyranny of majority opinion. In this light, exile becomes an essentially somatic experience, in which the subject's own body, or image, is appropriated by an external agency. Just as forced migration – mass or otherwise – threatens the autonomy of individuals by defining them in terms of economic value, so the commodification and expropriation of an individual's physical reality deprives her or him of the ability to live on her or his own terms.

The contributions that follow focus on the network of cultural, social, political and economic issues such as these to which the subject of exile gives rise. In order to provide insight into the multifaceted nature of exile, and understanding of the sorts of responses it engenders, a resolutely interdisciplinary approach has been adopted, and a range of different methodological perspectives have been chosen in order not only to illuminate the complex interpenetration of the historical and the contemporary, of suffering and opportunity, of memory and imagination, but also to demonstrate that interdisciplinarity itself offers an appropriate and productive means of gaining insight into the complex, transforming and challenging phenomenon of exile.

From the outset, one of the prime fascinations of the subject has been the paradox which lies at its heart: exile as manifestation of loss, suffering, and despair is also a concept which is creatively and intellectually stimulating. In an essay whose importance is highlighted by the number of references to it contained in this volume, Edward Saïd tellingly notes that exile is both 'a condition of terminal loss' and, at the same time, 'a potent, even enriching, motif of modern culture' (Saïd 2001: 173). By exploring themes and concepts of exile in relation to social experiences, to history and memory, to mappings and border crossings, to exclusion, change, and shifting identities, and to literature, photography, art, and film, this study will reflect this paradox. This multiplicity of forms, mirrored by the interdisciplinary perspectives from which they are considered, suggests not simply the pervasive nature of the subject but, in the rapidly evolving culture of postmodernity, the perilous and unstable – even exilic – relationship between reader and text, spectator and image.

Any division of the theme of exile into categories can, of course, only be provisional, given the fluid and interconnected relationship between the varieties of human experience it represents. The three sections into which the book is divided – space, time, and the body – reflect, however, the dominant preoccupations of the essays grouped within them and suggest a coherent progression from the marginalities and dislocations of spatial movement, through the unsettling interactions of time and memory, to the core of the exilic experience focused on the body.

In Part One, Carrie Tarr's essay on exile and displacement in the cinema of the French-Algerian-Gypsy filmmaker Tony Gatlif exposes in particularly acute form the impact of spatial exile and marginality. What is at issue here is not a single historical expulsion or retreat to a distant land but the perennial exile that results from the marginalisation and persecution of a community and a culture whose nomadic life is at odds with the historically fixed territories it inhabits. Whilst the Gypsies constitute one of the oldest cultural social groups in Europe, they have nevertheless always been defined as 'other' within its borders, considered inherently inferior, and ostracised and/ or persecuted precisely because they are not seen to belong to a 'nation'. Gypsies thus provide a graphic example of a group of people who are systematically criminalised, and condemned to remain at the fringes of society, by virtue of their ethnic identity. Looking at two of Gatlif's films in particular,

Les Princes (1983), and *Gadjo dilo* (1998), Tarr examines their
depictions of the absolute 'otherness' of Gypsy culture, and of
the prejudice and intolerance shown to them by 'respectable'
citizens, and by social and state institutions in general. The
sombre images and grim setting of the concrete estate in the
desolate outskirts of Paris, where Nara and his family are
briefly housed before being brutally evicted in *Les Princes*, and
the flat and inhospitable, snow-covered roads of Romania in
Gadjo dilo (the final part of Gatlif's 'Gypsy Trilogy') vividly
depict the marginalisation of the group, and the fragility and
instability of their status. Both films may perhaps be seen as
an elegy and, at the same time, a lament for the cultural traditions of the nomadic Gypsy. As Gatlif himself comments, in
what is perhaps yet another example of an internalisation of
the physical and historical experience of exile, 'their identity is
the only country the Roma people possess' (Morier 1998).

   If Simon Rattle chose *Leaving Home* as the title of his study
of twentieth-century music, it is a notion which could equally
well be applied to all cultural forms in a century in which
identity, like history, has been irrevocably shaped by exile, displacement, and the loss of certainty. Nowhere can this trend
be more clearly identified than in European cinema whose
long-standing concern with the exploration and articulation
of identity is increasingly approached through the device of
journey, with its self-conscious portrayal of movement,
change, and the transgression of frontier and frame. With particular reference to the Icelandic film, *Cold Fever* (Fridrik Thor
Fridriksson, 1994), Wendy Everett examines ways in which the
physical displacement involved in the journey of a stranger
across a strange land reveals identity as an open-ended
process which is both articulated in, and constructed by, the
stories we tell ourselves. Examining *Cold Fever* as a European
version of the road movie, a quintessentially Hollywood genre,
Everett reveals the ways in which Fridriksson's subversive and
self-conscious narrative strategies enable him to construct yet
another journey whose route leads across the unmappable
topographies of the self to the creative whiteness of the screen.

   Catherine Lupton's exploration of the work of Chris Marker,
and specifically of his 1982 film *Sans Soleil*, focuses on the way
in which travel exemplifies varieties of exile, in both time and
space. The disorientating experiences of perpetual travel and
cross-cultural encounter are a familiar feature of Marker's
films and multimedia projects, provoking and highlighting his
consistent refusal to establish a centred authorial identity in

his work. Marker, for whom geographical displacement manifests itself as dispersed subjectivity, is thus seen as an archetypal figure of contemporary intellectual interest in exile. This fascination with movements across geopolitical space in Marker's works is interwoven with his consuming preoccupation with memory, and the constellation of different orders of time. Lupton examines Marker's use of geographical displacement as a means of figuring an experience of temporal and historical exile, suggesting that the decentred subjectivity which emerges is not so much 'out of place' as 'out of time'. Central to this exploration is Marker's interest in new media – prefigured in the concluding 'Zone' section of *Sans Soleil* – and the possibilities they offer for translating literal journeys as virtual ones. Contrary to the widespread assumption that new technologies are in some sense inimical to the process of remembering, Marker values the distorting effects of digital and virtual media as the most appropriate means of conveying in representation the fundamental inaccessibility of the past.

The inaccessibility of the past similarly emerges as the central preoccupation of Georges Perec's and Robert Bober's documentary exploration of European migration to the United States, the subject of the chapter by Peter Wagstaff that opens the second section. In *Récits d'Ellis Island: histoires d'errance et d'espoir*, a thoughtful and moving film essay from 1980 on the trauma of exile and abandonment, Perec focuses on the dilapidated Ellis Island immigrant reception centre as an emblem of loss and disorientation, setting his own personal quest for a past and an identity against the broader canvas. In a complex interweaving of past and present, still and moving images, he posits the impossibility of recreating the past and the difficulty of coming to terms with that past in the present, relying instead on a terse and understated filmic narrative and a telling juxtaposition of past and present images. Searching for ways to express the inexpressible core of identity and loss, Perec contrasts the arrival of European migrants in the New World with the history of his own family, whose migration remained within the borders of Europe, and ended at Auschwitz. In creating unsettling, allusive correspondences between the methods used on Ellis Island to sort and codify migrants, and the triage techniques employed in the extermination camps of Europe, Perec's narrative constitutes a displacement of personal traumatic and irreversible exile, from family, past, and memory itself.

The shadow of mid-century Middle Europe hangs heavily, too, over the work of Arnold Daghani, whose visual re-workings of the experience of war-time deportation, imprisonment, and exile in Romania and the Ukraine are analysed by Deborah Schultz. Drawing on the extensive archive of Daghani's work at the University of Sussex, Schultz examines the relationship between forced migration and the workings of involuntary memory, with regard to representations of this relationship in the visual arts. In sharp contrast to Perec, however, Daghani experiences and responds to a constant interplay of past and present, through a range of interconnected memories – from the homeland, from previous places of exile, as well as short-term memories from the present place of residence, all of which change over time, in turn becoming more prominent or receding further as they are overlaid by experiences in the present. Visual works were continually remade by Daghani, and diaries were rewritten with ever more details remembered over time so that, while his work is very much located in the place in which it is made, the past and present of his experiences coexist at every level. Essentially fluid and mobile memories thus form their own ever-changing sequences and run at their own speeds, sometimes quickly, at other times in slow motion or repetitively. In this way, the relationship between external circumstances and internal memory, between absence and presence, are juxtaposed and constantly interact with each other. Above all, although memories may be called up at will, they often impose themselves upon the mind by force, appearing and reappearing, so that the past becomes a persistent component of the present. In this way, Schultz argues, the forced state of exile is closely reflected in the involuntary nature of memory.

If the functioning of memory resides in the desire to make the absent present – whether, as in the case of Perec, a forlorn hope or, as with Daghani, a repetitive overlayering of memory and experience – the experiments of the Belgian filmmaker Chantal Akerman offer a fascinating insight into the relationship between the human desire for a stable location through memory and the problematic status of the moving image. Lieve Spaas explores this edgy interface initially by underlining the contrast between the stability of the still photographic image, with its apparent access to a durable view of self, and the essential transience of the moving image. She raises the question as to whether film merely embeds the viewer's sense of exile from selfhood, or transfigures that sense to provide a response to the fractured visual experiences of our digitised, multimedia environment. Much of Akerman's early work reflects a wish to address the impact of the 'plethora of tantalising images' that prompt a sense of exile in the viewer. The use of the fixed, immobile camera and lengthy shots leads both to a refusal to interpret and a determination to produce an awareness of the ways in which the fast-moving images to which film accustoms the viewer result in a visual distortion which is itself a form of exile. Akerman's later work integrates this preoccupation with a formal, visual exile and a more traditional geographical displacement. Her family background, with its experience of displacement between Eastern and Western Europe, is repeatedly evoked, and extended to embrace the exile of Eastern European Jews in New York and indeed the twentieth-century diaspora as a whole. Most striking of all Akerman's explorations of visual exile is perhaps *D'Est* (1993), in which a multimedia installation of simultaneous film projection and multiple television images confronts the viewer with a fragmented view echoing the fragmentation of exile itself.

The faculty of memory is also central to the work of Scottish filmmaker Bill Douglas, whose haunting autobiographical *Trilogy* juxtaposes the experience of physical exile in a historical context with the intimate narratives of his own childhood estrangement from community, even family. Christine Sprengler shows how Douglas, by privileging the individual over the collective, focuses on the ways in which personal history is excluded from the broader canvas of History as it is habitually understood and envisioned. It is striking that a filmmaker notorious for his obsessive attention to the precise recreation of those concrete details, images and events that make up his memories of childhood should choose to foreground an entirely invented character, whose fictional presence as a German prisoner in war-time Scotland functions metaphorically through his status as an exile from both his own physical homeland and Douglas's autobiographical veracity. The unstable status of this early replacement father figure for the young Jamie/Bill Douglas raises intriguing questions about the level of his fictionality, as an invention of the mature filmmaker for aesthetic reasons or as imaginative creation of the child. By bringing together the personal and the historically-grounded collective memories that clearly privilege the notion of exile in its conventional (spatial) sense, Douglas can be seen to reveal a desire to censure his community for repeatedly exiling him both physically and emotionally and for making what ought to be familiar – his home – an essentially unfamiliar locus of estrangement and alienation.

The idea of exile as estrangement and alienation is easily apprehended at the level of geographical dislocation or temporal displacement: forced from home, divorced from the past, the exile can find no solid ground. Of increasing urgency in late twentieth- and early twenty-first century thinking, however, is consideration of the body itself as a contested terrain. Gabriele Griffin, in 'Exile and the Body', the first chapter of the third section, contends that the body, configured as a site or location, no longer occupies a naturalised or uncontentious place. Subjectivity and the body no longer necessarily coincide; the body as site has thus become a place of exile, from which or into which subjectivities are ushered. Fundamental to Griffin's argument is the awareness that exile, far from being an abstract concept, is in fact founded in somatic realities: it is, she argues, about pain. This argument is persuasively advanced through a discussion of five categories of 'subjugated subjectivities', which include: the atrocities of rape and torture as an instrument of political repression and domination, sexual abuse in non-war situations, the commodification of the female body in the culture of late capitalism, the representation of HIV/AIDS, the experience of racism. In each instance it is overwhelmingly clear from Griffin's account that the least satisfactory response is what she calls 'the triumphalist narrative of overcoming'. Far more significant is the response adumbrated by Julia Kristeva, who argues for 'a reconciliation of self and other, a recognition of the strangeness that resides both within the self and the other'. The exile may recover, but will never heal.

This intimate correlation of outer and inner worlds is central to an understanding of Leslie Feinberg's novel *Stone Butch Blues*. In a subtle analysis, Feroza Basu brings together the concepts of physical displacement through travel, and transsexuality. In a text variously defined as transgendered fiction, fictionalised autobiography and lesbian literature, the narrator of Feinberg's novel describes her experiences in terms of both journey and exile. At issue, in particular, is the phenomenon of exile from, and return to, a gendered physical body, in that the transgendered narrating subject is seen in terms of metaphorical exile and actual physical displacement. Here North American society is depicted, in contradistinction to Baudrillard's image of a 'zone of sexual permissiveness', as brutally intolerant of transsexuality. Recent theories in the field of cultural geography offer the proposition that the body itself be considered as a constitutive part of physical space, and this in turn permits a view of exile based on the body as a site of travel, within which the mind seeks to find its home location. In Feinberg's novel, the narrator's body is seen as a zone within which various forms of microdisplacement can take place: subjectivity is a consciousness contained within an alterable physical exterior. As that body is also most at ease, in safety, during actual physical travel – by train or, ideally, motorcycle – the novel cuts across traditional definitions of home in chronological or cartographic terms. Basu argues that such definitions are too firmly rooted in heteronormative conceptions of home, denying the multiple possibilities of movement within the inner and outer geographies of the body.

An interpretation of exile within theories of social action forms the basis for Chris Horrocks's analysis of the performative stances of Andy Warhol. The image of Warhol as an ambiguous, peripheral character, 'strangely present and absent' is examined in the context of theories of displacement, disidentification and role distancing, seen as strategies employed to destabilise and reconstitute norms and rules of social interaction. A constant evaluation and awareness of his relationship, both physical and mental, with the world around him enable Warhol to exploit his 'otherness' so as to reorder each social context on his own terms. Responding to an interviewer's questions with alternate 'yes' and 'no' answers enables Warhol slyly to refocus attention on the normative codes of the situation in which he is placed, while simultaneously distancing himself and appearing to conform. Blurring all distinctions and categories in this manner makes it increasingly difficult to decide whether it is the individual who is exiled from the enveloping social framework, or the reverse.

The final chapter of *Cultures of Exile* also draws on concepts of the norm, and on deviations from it, in relation to repesentations of the human body in visual, specifically photographic terms. Richard Sawdon Smith's experience as a practising photographer provides striking evidence for the limited awareness of, and tolerance for images of the body which contravene the normative and the socially acceptable. Such limitations have profound implications for, as Sawdon Smith explains, 'Issues of sexuality, gender and self-identity are bound up within photographic representations, as are issues of ideology, politics and power'. The starting-point for his analysis of these issues is a series of photographs of a friend with AIDS – photographs intended to document the physical changes to which he was subject. The selection of one such image as the winning portrait in a photographic competition, coupled with the refusal of the competition's media sponsor to publish it, prompts a sustained reflection on the apparently uncrossable border between what is seen as normal and what is seen as abnormal, or diseased. Examples of other photographic work, both by and of the disabled and diseased, suggest that the exile from normality which has become the lot of anyone failing to conform to society's expectations of the healthy body, can be challenged, since photography is a medium which requires the viewer to fill in and contextualise images in order to make sense of them. Writing about society and disability is too frequently rooted in a normalised sensibility which prevents identification with or understanding of anything beyond the scope of that norm, so that the marginalised or excluded are simply observed, classified, controlled. In enabling the spectator to confront sober and truthful images, rather than colluding in the construction of a barrier that excludes, the photographer can contribute to a reassessment of the 'abnormal' which is not exiled from normality.

Most of the cultural expressions of exile which have formed the basis for analysis in this volume have as a fundamental premise, whether explicit or implicit, the need to question and re-examine notions of heterogeneity, fragmentation, and the difficulty of access or return to an ontological centre, the place 'where distance no longer counts' (Berger 1984: 91). It would be invidious, therefore, to attempt to coax or coerce an overarching thematic unity from what follows, beyond that of the sense of loss, absence and dislocation, all of which are inscribed within the word 'exile'. And yet the mere existence, the necessary creation of these written, filmed, photographed, painted, sketched, performed expressions and impressions of exile(s) perhaps prompts a consideration of Saïd's assertion, echoing Adorno, 'that the only home truly available now, though fragile and vulnerable, is in writing' (Saïd 2001: 184). Not just writing, of course, but all the mobile, transformative, inexhaustible forms of expression available to the creative mind.

It is therefore evident that the concepts of exile and displacement, which loom so large and exert such fascination in contemporary thought and culture, resist and reject any form of polarisation or neat definition. Seizing and exploring these contrasting, often contradictory aspects of exile, the essays that follow, each of which examines in some way 'the perilous territory of not-belonging' (Saïd 2001:177), make a stimulating, wide-ranging, and important contribution to a vital and continuing debate.

References

Morier, R. (1998) 'History's scapegoats', www.oneworld.org/ni/ issue266/contents.htm

Saïd, E. W. (2001) *Reflections on Exile and Other Literary and Cultural Essays*, London: Granta Books.

PART I

SPACE

EXILE AND DISPLACEMENT IN THE CINEMA OF TONY GATLIF: *LES PRINCES* (1983) AND *GADJO DILO* (1998)

Carrie Tarr

The figure of the Gypsy/Rom has become increasingly prominent in European media representations of the 1990s, in part
perhaps as a result of their presence among the migrants and
refugees currently making their way from East to West after
the break up of the Soviet Union and the disintegration of
Yugoslavia, in part too because of the vivid hold they have on
the Western imagination as emblematic figures of nomadicity
and alterity. Members of a race living, as it were, in near-
constant flight and exile (Andrew 2001: 16), they have been
the perennial victims of racial hostility and persecution (from
their incorporation into slavery in fifteenth-century Bulgaria
and their planned extermination by the Nazis in the Second
World War to recent pogroms in countries such as Hungary
and Romania). Their ethnic difference and their cultural sep-
aratism and distrust of others (the *gadje* or non-Gypsies) have
helped make them scapegoats for social and political unrest in
the countries in which they find themselves, whether it be the
post-Communist Eastern block or the more affluent countries
of Western Europe. Though the Gypsy may be romanticised in
Western fiction as the embodiment of freedom, the projection

of the repressed desires of the over-civilised West, according to Isabel Fonseca they are more often perceived as 'the quintessential outsiders of the European imagination: sinister, separate, literally dark, and synonymous with sorcery and crime' (Fonseca 1996: 273). Solutions to the perceived 'Gypsy problem' have conventionally been sought either in their expulsion beyond national (or other) boundaries or in attempts at enforced assimilation through sedentarisation. However, despite the fact that the Gypsy population of Europe has been increasingly obliged to accept sedentarisation since the end of the Second World War, their apparent lack of a country of origin and their perceived disrespect for boundaries and borders continue to challenge dominant desires for national integrity and stability.

Lacking a homeland, the Gypsies themselves invest their identity in their cultural difference. 'After all', as French-Algerian-Gypsy filmmaker Tony Gatlif has said, 'their identity is the only country the Roma people possess' (Morier 1998). Paradoxically, then, while their perceived preference for nomadic displacement and their actual displacement (for some) as refugees may make them appear emblematic of the postmodern condition, their fear of and resistance to hybridisation through contact with *gadje* continues to set them apart.[1] Yet at the same time, their survival through the centuries has often depended on their ability to adapt and change, and they are not impermeable to the forces of acculturation brought about by sedentarisation.

This paper looks at shifts in the construction of place and identity in two films by Tony Gatlif,[2] focusing on the tensions provoked by sedentarisation first in *Les Princes* (1983), set among a community of Gypsies in France, and then in *Gadjo dilo* (1998), set among a community of Gypsies in Romania.[3] As a Gypsy filmmaker, Gatlif is openly concerned to defend Gypsies and make films that they might be 'proud of' (Morier 1998) (though in the process he is arguably contravening 'the Gypsy way', not just because the transmission of Gypsy culture traditionally depends on oral storytelling, music, song and dance, but also because of taboos against collaboration with *gadje*). Nevertheless, his cultural interventions target a *gadje* audience in a medium that has conventionally either demonised the Gypsy as the almost subhuman, diabolical other, or romanticised the Gypsy as the exotic, larger than life embodiment of freedom and passion. Gatlif has proclaimed his awareness of the fact that the image of the Gypsy is the product of 'five centuries of prejudice' and his aim to demystify this image by drawing attention to 'the richness and complexity of the realities of Roma existence', including the racist violence and hostility to which they are frequently subjected (Gatlif 1998).

Consequently, there are significant moments of self reflexivity in each of the films considered here, where Gatlif demonstrates how the Gypsy stereotype is manufactured and perpetuated by the dominant culture (and also assumed by the Gypsy at times when it suits him). In *Les Princes*, when a couple of absurd tourists stop to take pictures of the distressed Gypsy family and their campfire by the roadside, Gypsy hero Nara refuses to be treated as picturesque local colour, beats the man up and destroys his camera and film. Later, when an equally caricatural German journalist asks him standard questions about his origins and culture but shows no interest in the hardship of his life in the *banlieue*, he starts playing to stereotype and shocks her into silence by telling her he wants to make love to her. Although it could be argued that these scenes simply confirm the stereotype of the Gypsy as a figure of menace and sexual aggression, the focus on Nara's narrative and subjective point of view invites the audience to sympathise with his reaction to the *gadje's* attempts to objectify and exoticise him. In *Gadjo dilo*, the young French hero, Stéphane, is shown silencing his animated female Gypsy companion in order to achieve a pure sound recording of some Gypsy musicians; but at the end he performs a ritualised destruction and burial of all his music recordings, belatedly demonstrating his realisation that they encourage people to reify and fetishise Gypsy culture, rather than genuinely engage with it.

Nevertheless, Gatlif himself can still be accused of succumbing to a romanticised view of the Gypsy community he wishes to represent, even though these films draw on an apparently authentic cast and material, and are set within a specific contemporary, sociohistorical context. The two films work over the options facing Gypsies when life on the road has come to an end, the threat of the loss of the specificity of Gypsy culture through the processes of acculturation in France in the early 1980s (in *Les Princes*), their continued repression if they seek to retain and flaunt their specificity in post-Ceaucescu Romania (in *Gadjo dilo*). However, both options centre on the experiences of a romanticised male Gypsy, a traditional paterfamilias whose colourful visual impact and emotional and physical excesses contrast with the colourless appearance and cold, heartless behaviour of the stereotyped *gadje*.[4] In *Les Princes*, Nara is an attractive, swarthy man, always dressed in a hat, wearing a colourful shirt and tie and ornate belt and rings; he is frequently shot from a slight upward angle, and is always on the move, doing a deal, getting in and out of trouble. In *Gadjo dilo*, Izidor is an imposing, craggy, patriarchal figure, who stands out from the crowd with his hat and beard, his loud voice, his sharp suits and his hyperbolic language and gestures. The affective centre of the films thus risks becoming a celebration of and mourning for a timeless archetype of Gypsy identity, rather than directly addressing the present-day concerns in which the characters are embedded, and the need for adaptation and change.

In each of these films, the fate of Gypsy culture and identity is played out within a narrative trajectory that begins with the Gypsy returning to a sedentary home, but ends with bereavement, loss and displacement. The rest of this paper will therefore examine the relationship between space and identity within and across the two films, including the use of music and dance to construct temporary but unstable spaces of collective belonging and identity.

Les Princes

Les Princes is concerned with three generations of a Gypsy family who have been allocated a flat in a *cité de transit* on the periphery of Paris.[5] The block of flats is a site of grim, concrete desolation, humanised only by the presence of children (including children of African-Caribbean origin) and a white horse, which Nara is trying to sell. The area round about consists of a wasteland on which are parked a few Gypsy caravans, a bar called 'Le Bar des Princes', and a vast, deserted factory near a railway line, which neatly points to the contemporary problem of unemployment and explains the need for people on the periphery to scrape together a living by whatever means possible. The mise-en-scène of the block of flats and its surroundings is characterised by a poetic realist style, focusing on the rubble, rain, desolation and darkness, and punctuated by a madman hollering each night for 'Madeleine'. The interior of the block is similarly depressing, with its cracked walls, peeling paint and sawn-off banisters. But the Gypsy's flat itself provides a colourful contrast, with its painted walls and well-stocked fridge (admittedly with a broken door). At the same time, the fragile boundary between outside and inside is persistently challenged by Nara's mother, who protests against her enforced sedentarisation by insisting on keeping the windows open, provoking constant argument with Nara until, in exasperation, he tears them down and takes them off to sell.

The effects of sedentarisation on the family's identity as Gypsies are primarily reflected in the changes affecting Nara's womenfolk. Miralda, his wife, despite her traditional appearance and deference to her menfolk, is apparently taking the pill on the advice of a social worker (against the Gypsy way); and his only child, Zorka, is enjoying school and is top of her class (and has been teaching her grandmother to read and write). The film opens on a family crisis brought about by Nara's response to his wife's behaviour, since Nara has thrown her out (he wants to remarry and have lots of children), the police have picked her up for loitering, and Miralda, desperate to see her daughter, is reduced to hiding in the desolate, deserted spaces of the wasteland. The crisis spreads to embrace Miralda's somewhat caricatural three brothers (including Gatlif himself in a knife-wielding cameo role), who want to resolve their sister's position, by violence if necessary, and Zorka, whom Nara forcibly removes from school because he doesn't want her tainted by a French education (he himself is illiterate).

Nara's identity crisis is compounded by his inability (or unwillingness) to pay his bills, which, as his mother predicts, eventually leads to the family's brutal eviction from their flat. Until that point, the film charts Nara's various attempts to make money: selling a horse, caning chairs, stealing cable from a disused factory, and working on a building site until his family problems cause him to be fired. Though his activities are mostly confined to the spaces of the periphery, he also makes trips into the city, one of which leads to a racist attack (he follows Zorka's elegant, blonde schoolteacher into town and is subsequently attacked by her husband and fellow racists in a bar, a situation from which he manages to escape, though not without nearly getting pissed on as he hides under a car); however, he is also subject to racist violence in the *banlieue*, as when he falls out with his *gadjo* friend Petitpon (they disagree on the morality of stealing from an old lady), who then has him beaten up (though Petitpon in turn is beaten up and humiliated by knife-wielding Nara). Nara's principal refuge from the trials and tribulations of his existence is the space of the Bar des Princes, where his identity is restored and confirmed through his drinking, the melancholy laments of the Gypsy musicians, his conversations with Bijou, the prostitute, who is dying of consumption, and his sexual relationship with Fatima, the woman who runs the bar. All these encounters show him to be a man of immense pride, physicality, violence, energy and emotionality.

The scene of the family's eviction constitutes a turning point in the narrative, and highlights the film's critique of the French authorities and their vicious treatment of the Gypsies. Significantly, the film cuts directly from their eviction to a contrasting scene of Gypsy community, in which music, dance, and song create a space of shared pleasure and confirmation of identity, underlined by panning shots of the women's faces and brightly coloured skirts, scarves, and earrings. But this insert scene occupies a timeless space not directly linked to the narrative (like the opening credit sequence which focuses on a Gypsy toddler chewing on some money bills amid a scene of mud and desolation); it is followed in turn by the police torching the wooden hut in which the family have taken shelter at night (and which has been condemned because it is not a fixed dwelling). Their double expulsion sets in motion the second part of the film, in which the crazy grandmother, protesting at their being treated like 'rats' and demanding 'respect and understanding', sets off on the road on foot, determined to find a lawyer to support their cause; she is followed reluctantly by Nara, and even more reluctantly by Zorka and, at a distance, by the rejected wife and her three brothers in their red Mercedes. What the spectator sees is not a comforting recreation of Gypsy community on the road, but a disturbingly fragmented, dysfunctional family, separated by gender and generation. Indeed, the mise-en-scène of the long, flat, empty country road suggests that it is actually little better than the *banlieue* they have left behind, since it is characterised by constant rain and mud, a village with a burnt-out factory wasteland, and a Gypsy campsite located specifically on the local rubbish dump.

Nevertheless, the road provides the opportunity for the Gypsies to consolidate their identity in relation to the *gadje*, as in the sequence set in a smart restaurant (L'Auberge du Cheval Blanc) where Nara has a rendezvous with a German journalist (recommended to him by the bourgeois couple who employed him to re-cane their chairs). The manager tries unsuccessfully to eject Nara, but Nara disrupts the interview, and dances on the money the journalist throws at him, and his wife's brothers arrive and beat up the manager. Meanwhile the grandmother steals cheese from the restaurant, plays tricks on the police by telling their fortunes, and then breaks into a house in the village where she consumes a huge platter of unattended couscous royal (while the white bourgeois couple are quarrelling in the next room). Zorka, too, tricks a grocer and runs off with a Camembert, leaving the field clear for her father to steal some more. But she does so after telling the grocer that she is NOT a nomad and wants to be a vet when she grows up, and she subsequently protests to Nara that she does not want to be a thief. So the family divisions remain, and Nara continues to ignore Miralda, until the grandmother's collapse by the roadside in the pouring rain finally obliges him to ask her for help. The grandmother's death thus enables mother and daughter to come together at last, and the final shot of the sequence foregrounds their embrace, while grief-stricken Nara is relegated to the background.

However, the film is still unable to resolve differences within the family, and ends instead on a very different note. The dying grandmother had earlier asked her son to transmit her notebooks to her lawyer and then to bury them with her, and we can assume, as spectators, that these notebooks contain her writings about her life as a Gypsy (she has already mentioned that she lost fourteen children in the Nazi death camps). The final sequence cuts first to what is presumably her burial site, then to a series of shots of a procession of Gypsies with their dancing bears and ponies, which eventually moves out beyond the field of vision. The sequence is not clearly integrated into the fiction (and may or may not include Nara and his family), but apparently constitutes a tribute to the old lady and her desire to memorialise a traditional form of Gypsy culture that may be dying with her. Having demonstrated that for Nara and family, however desperate their life in the *banlieue*, being on the road is no longer either a possible or a desirable option, the film can only find the wandering Gypsy a place in fantasy. Rather than persisting in its critique of French society and its analysis of the contradictions facing the modern Gypsy family eking out a living on the urban periphery, the film becomes an elegy for the nomadic life that once gave Gypsies their identity, an elegy that is first introduced in the opening credit sequence by the musical lament whose repeated use punctuates the film and accompanies the final sequence.

Gadjo dilo

The second film of Gatlif's so-called Gypsy trilogy (for which he was awarded the Prix des Amériques in Montréal in 1998) was *Latcho Drom/Safe Journey* (1993), a striking documentary which traces the history of Gypsy migration and the suffering of the Roma people through episodic scenes of music, song and dance, set in various countries from India through to Spain. *Gadjo dilo* marks a return to an individual narrative of Gypsy life, but not to the contemporary situation in Western Europe. Rather it opts for the more remote and 'exotic' setting of rural Romania, which allows Gatlif to represent a more 'primitive' form of Gypsy existence than in *Les Princes*. Arguably, then, the film's very setting invites nostalgia for a way of life that is under threat.

The film begins and ends on a road that appears to be just as flat and inhospitable as that of *Les Princes*, covered in snow and leading nowhere in particular. However, this time the man on the road is Stéphane, a young Parisian, not a Gypsy, who has abandoned his home and family in order to track down Gypsy singer Nora Luca (because her poignant singing was repeatedly played by his father on his deathbed). And this time the traditional Gypsies sighted on the road are integrated into the fiction. However, the decision to structure the film's narrative around Stéphane means that the film falls rather conventionally into the Eurocentric tradition of approaching the ethnic Other, in this case a Romanian Gypsy community, through the eyes of a white West European male. Gatlif's choice of protagonist is a measure, perhaps, of his concerns about his own relationship to the topic he is addressing (as a successfully integrated Gypsy), and of his desire to find ways of making the topic accessible and palatable for a *gadje* audi- ence. Its effects are mitigated in part by the fact that Stéphane (Romain Duris), the eponymous 'gadjo dilo' (crazy foreigner), is initially the object of the gaze of the Gypsies he meets; and the film subsequently strives to represent the points of view of both Gypsy and *gadjo* in order to construct a series of privi- leged (and often comic) moments of linguistic and cultural exchange between them. Nevertheless, the film ends as it begins, with Stéphane's experiences, which demonstrate how his life has been enriched by his encounter with the exotic Other (he has been adopted by a surrogate Gypsy father figure and acquired a Gypsy lover). It is less clear that the Gypsy community itself benefits from their contact with him, since the narrative of cultural exchange ends somewhat ambiguously (as discussed below) and is in any case intercut with a more melodramatic narrative of violence and revenge between Gypsies and Romanians that ends in tragedy, and in which Stéphane plays no part other than as horrified observer.

Stéphane's wild hair, gaping shoes and eccentric behaviour (in the opening sequence the camera repeatedly turns through 360° following his point of view as he whirls round in the road), make him an object of curiosity for others. A group of laughing Gypsy women on the back of a cart (including Sabina, his future lover) assail him with lascivious insults (whose meanings are available through subtitles to the audience, but not to Stéphane himself). Outside a Romanian village bar that has closed for the night, an elderly, drunken Gypsy, Izidor, whose son, Adriani, has been denounced by the Romanian villagers and taken away by the police, seizes on Stéphane as a gift from God to help him drown his sorrows in a bottle of vodka. Stéphane's subsequent confrontation with the Gypsy community gives spectators identifying with a French point of view the opportunity of experiencing what it is like not to understand what is going on and to be treated as Other by an initially fearful and hostile population (the Gypsies accuse him of being a giant, a thief, a child snatcher and a murderer and want him to go back where he comes from). However, his expansive behaviour, his desire to communicate and his interest in Roma language and culture quickly earn him a position as Izidor's adopted son. Stéphane never manages to find Nora Luca, though he keeps on trying, but instead finds himself in the privileged position of being accepted into the Gypsy community.

His encounter with the Gypsies is above all a catalyst for scenes that enable Gatlif to represent the persistence of the Gypsy way of life, albeit a romanticised, pre-modern version of it. Unlike *Les Princes*, there are no internal challenges to Gypsy traditions: poverty and alcoholism do not seem to have any noticeable effects on the group's internal cohesion, Izidor's authority is never seriously called into question, and even though Sabina, his niece, is stigmatised for having left her husband in Belgium, she is apparently free to lead a fairly independent life. The extended family dwells on the periphery of the village close to the forest, in a sprawling encampment consisting of Izidor's single-storey house with hayloft, outbuildings and tents, and various neighbouring houses, where the boundary between indoors and outdoors is fairly fluid (much of the communal activity takes place out of doors, as in the scene of music making that greets Adriani's release from prison). The film documents the Gypsies' activities, stressing their industry, ingenuity, and hospitality: the women gather wood and provide food, the children teach Stéphane the language, the men mend pots and pans and later his clapped out car, and divert electricity to give him a light. Cultural differences such as the Gypsies' disapproval of Stéphane's attempts to tidy up Izidor's home (a woman's job) and lack of understanding of his fixation on Nora Luca (there are so many other singers) are smoothed over through the use of music that creates spaces of shared pleasures. Stéphane makes Izidor a homemade phonograph that enables him to listen to a recording of his father's music, Izidor takes Stéphane to a Gypsy wedding where he and his family are performing, and later Sabina escorts Stéphane in his search for recordings of Gypsy musicians. Live music and dance express the Gypsies' identity and underline their emotionality, sensuality and excess, which find further expression in their crude, outspoken language and their freely expressed sexual desires. After their outing to a Bucharest nightclub, where Stéphane expresses himself in Gypsy dancing, Izidor has to be restrained from forcing Sabina to have sex against her will, and Sabina initiates a passionate sexual relationship with Stéphane who has proved that his language and desire match hers. Unlike desperate, haunted Miralda in *Les Princes*, Sabina is articulate and sure of herself, her status enabling her to pursue her own desires whilst at the same time embodying a romanticised vision of primitive Gypsyness, with her wild, vibrant language and dancing, her colourful appearance (including her hair plaited with gold coins) and her closeness to nature, embodied in the shots of her washing half-naked in the tent, and running naked in the woods with Stéphane.

The film thus glosses over inequalities and disagreements within the Gypsy community (there are no signs of the children getting an education or the women objecting to their roles), and especially the question of their economic situation (the family seem able to make a living from their music making and other jobs). Instead it calls attention to the fragility and instability of their status in Romania, which explains and justifies their need for a coherent sense of identity and community. In his lament for his imprisoned son, Izidor proclaims that there is no justice for Gypsies in Romania; later scenes demonstrate that the Gypsies do not expect to receive proper medical treatment; and Sabina tells Stéphane (who is taking notes) about the violence against Gypsies at the time of the Ceaucescu regime. But racial hostility is most clearly demonstrated through the Gypsies' interactions with the native Romanians in the interior of the austere, unfriendly bar in the nearby Romanian village, outside which Stéphane had first met Izidor. Izidor's return to show off Stéphane as his adopted son, and his provocative visionary tirade declaring that Gypsies in France enjoy positions of authority in the community and live in harmony with the French (an ironic touch on Gatlif's part), provoke the obvious invitation to go off and join them. Adriani's return to gloat at his release from prison is met in turn by insults from a grim, inhospitable Romanian villager, and when Adriani hurls a glass in his face, the man accidentally falls to his death. In a climactic scene of revenge, the Romanian villagers seek to rid themselves of the Gypsy 'pestilence' by destroying Izidor's house and surrounding dwellings, torching the tents and the hayloft where Adriani has sought refuge, and driving the other Gypsies present to take flight in the woods. The sequence (which has a basis in contemporary events, see Fonseca 1996) suggests that sedentarisation in post-Ceaucescu Romania has not led to acculturation and that the future of the authentic Gypsy community lies, as in the past, in death, bereavement and exile.

The film concludes without placing the event in a wider political context and relating it to the contemporary issue of Gypsy migration from Romania. After a last shot of a grief-stricken Izidor bewailing the death of his son, it focuses on Stéphane back on the road, presumably returning to France, but stopping in order to destroy his notebook and the tape recordings he has made, an ending that is radically different from that of *Les Princes*. Stéphane carefully buries his accumulated knowledge of Gypsy history and music by the side of the road and lays a vodka bottle on the site, reprising the actions of Izidor earlier in the film when he was mourning the death of a musician friend. However, the meanings of this act are not completely clear. On the one hand, following the destruction of the Gypsy encampment, it can be seen to represent a general mourning for what is happening to Gypsy culture, especially as Stéphane's last image of Izidor and family making music (at the time of Adriani's death at Romanian hands) was for the benefit of a Romanian family who were raucously singing the Nora Luca song that has haunted him throughout (and that accompanies the shots of his discovery, with Sabina, of the burnt-out settlement). On the other, perhaps Stéphane's rite of passage means that he has finally understood that he does not need to objectify Gypsy culture through cultural arte-facts, since he has internalised it in his own behaviour and emotional life. The film ends with Stéphane performing a Gypsy dance in the middle of the road, recalling both his own spinning round in the empty road at the beginning of the film and the ritual dance performed by Izidor at his friend's grave. Meanwhile the film cuts to show an apparently tamed Sabina on the back seat of the car, looking on with an approving, if not altogether appropriate smile, indicating perhaps that there is an alternative to homelessness and that it lies in throwing in one's lot with the *gadje* Other. Despite the film's basically essentialist (and romantic) vision of Gypsy identity, then, it also recognises that the future depends on some sort of hybridisation, in this case through Sabina's association with an appropriately crazy, Gypsified *gadjo*.

However, if Stéphane has discovered that his personal engagement with Sabina and with Gypsy life is more impor-tant than his documentation of it for others, his act of appar-ent vandalism paradoxically calls into question Gatlif's own position in making films about Gypsies (and the spectator's for viewing them). For surely the documentation of Gypsy life is precisely what Gatlif aims to do, in *Gadjo dilo* as in *Les Princes*. The contradiction is apparent in the transition from the mournful silence accompanying Stéphane's dance to the lively non-diegetic Gypsy music that accompanies the closing cred-its. However, this transition can be read not so much as Gatlif's failure to address the issue of representation raised in the film (since *Gadjo Dilo* even more than *Les Princes* offers apparently unmediated access to authenticity), but rather as a reassertion of his fundamental romanticisation of Gypsy iden-tity, demonstrating what Stéphane may not yet have fully understood, namely, the ability of Gypsy culture to survive the vagaries of its history of exile.

Notes

1. Their lifestyle has been threatened by the enclosure of common land and the resistance of national governments to Gypsy migration patterns. It is also threatened by their loss of traditional crafts and means of employment.
2. Gatlif was born in the suburbs of Algiers in 1948 to a family of Gypsies from Andalucia. He came to France in 1962 (at the end of the Algerian War), was inspired by Michel Simon to train as an actor, worked at the Théâtre

National Populaire with Gérard Depardieu (among others) and subsequently progressed to writing and directing his own films.

3. Gatlif has directed about a dozen films to date, all of which focus on marginalised characters. *Mondo* (1996) and *Vengo* (2000) also focus on Gypsies.

4. In fact, Nara is played by Jewish *pied noir* actor Gérard Darmon, and his mother by veteran French stage actress Muse Dalbray. In *Gadjo dilo*, Sabine is played by Romanian actress Rona Hartner, alongside Romain Duris as Stéphane. Izidor Serban (Izidor) is thus the only Gypsy with a major role.

5. It is interesting to note that *Les Princes* was made before the 'Beur' films of the mid-1980s, and was one of the first French films to address the topic of the *banlieue*. It includes a number of tropes later used in *banlieue* films, e.g., the trip into the town centre which leads to abuse from French racists, the exclusion from the restaurant (later nightclubs), the presence of the white horse in the housing estate, police violence. One fundamental difference from the 'Beur' films though, is that Gatlif centres on the patriarchal figure and the culture he represents, whereas Beur filmmakers of the 1980s (who are of roughly the same age) identify with the second generation and their problems in negotiating their fractured identity.

References

Andrew, G. (2001) 'Seeking Sanctuary', National Film Theatre programme, June 2001.

Fonseca, I. (1996) *Bury Me Standing: The Gypsies and their Journey*, New York: Vintage.

Gatlif, T. (1998) Interview in *Télérama*, 8 April, 1998.

Morier, R. (1998) 'History's scapegoats', www.oneworld.org/ ni/issue266/contents.htm

CHAPTER 2

LEAVING HOME: EXILE AND DISPLACEMENT IN CONTEMPORARY EUROPEAN CINEMA

Wendy Everett

When Sir Simon Rattle was invited to create a series of television programmes for Channel Four, dealing with the history of twentieth-century music (his own 'conducted tour' of the twentieth century), he chose the title *Leaving Home*, not only because it reflected the fact that the century itself had been irrevocably shaped by journeys of migration and exile, both voluntary and forced, but also because it seemed to him to provide 'the dominant metaphor for a time in which all the certainties, social, political, intellectual, and artistic, [had] migrated' (quoted in Hall 1996: 1).

What Rattle's title therefore also reveals is his awareness that the corollary of the migratory experiences that so fundamentally marked the century is the metaphysical sense of homelessness that has increasingly come to be recognised as articulating the modern condition, what Martin Jesinghausen refers to, in an essay on Wenders, as 'the transcendental homelessness of modern life' (Jesinghausen 2000: 83).

An important consequence of the loss of belief in a fixed and unproblematical form of identity firmly rooted in place (home), is an increasing awareness that identity itself is essentially fluid and migratory; an on-going process which is both constructed and articulated through our own temporal and spatial journeys, and the stories we constantly tell ourselves.

The resulting insecurity may reasonably be understood as one of the principal reasons for the obsessive concern with memory and identity that dominated European cultural discourse of all kinds in the second half of the century.

One of the key forms of contemporary discourse is, of course, the cinema, which Rattle includes, alongside the motor car, aeroplane, telephone, wireless, vacuum cleaner, and gramophone record, in his list of inventions that provoked both the optimism and the fearful uncertainty that heralded the twentieth century, and thus helped to set in motion its journey into the unknown. But whilst it is undeniably true that all the above inventions did drastically transform our spatial and temporal geographies and identities, it is equally clear that film, in fact, goes much further than the others. As prime source of the images with which we make sense of the world and our role in it, as potent medium for reflecting our experiences, and telling our stories, film did not merely instigate the process of journey and change but, through its moving images, actually became part of that journey.

In turn, film itself has become obsessed by the theme of journey, as part of its self-conscious articulation of its own spatio-temporal language as much as its role as teller of contemporary stories, and creator of contemporary images. Accordingly, it is my intention in this essay to explore some of the ways in which filmic representations of journey may be seen to articulate the modern condition. Rather than focusing directly on the narratives of exile, displacement, immigration, and exclusion that feature so widely within contemporary European cinema's obsessive mapping and charting of twentieth century experiences, I have instead chosen to concentrate on the formal characteristics of the journey narrative as expression of contemporary (cinematic) identity. In other words, this essay will explore how by structuring narrative as journey, as the mobile negotiation of unfamiliar places, cultures, and identities, film is able not only to interrogate key issues of our time, but also to comment self-consciously upon its own role within them.

The European Road Movie

The most obvious manifestation of the cinematic journey is, of course, the road movie, a fluid and open-ended genre which uses the narrative trajectory of road as an extended metaphor of quest and discovery through which to approach fundamental concepts of identity. At the same time, the road movie self-consciously explores the relationship between the spatial and temporal displacement of journey and the discourse of film itself, and it is for that reason that the genre has been recognised as one of the most telling expressions of modernist and postmodern cinema (Deleuze 1986: 3–24). Moreover, given the road movie's origins as a peculiarly 'Hollywood genre that catches peculiarly American dreams, tensions, and anxieties' (Cohan and Hark 1997: 2), it is particularly interesting to explore ways in which contemporary European directors have so widely adopted this genre while ruthlessly subverting it from within so as to provide a telling commentary on the complex and multiple identities of European cinema. The extensive list of films which simultaneously exploit and subvert the road movie genre in this fashion might include, for example: *Leningrad Cowboys Go America* (Aki Kaurismäki, Finland, 1989); *Journey of Hope* (Xavier Koller, Turkey/Switzerland, 1990); *Dear Diary* (Nanni Moretti, Italy, 1994); *Trains 'N' Roses* (Peter Lichtefeld, Germany/Finland, 1997); *Last Resort* (Pawel Pawlikowski, UK, 2001), many films by Wim Wenders, but particularly *Alice in the Cities* (1974), *Kings of the Road* (1975), and *Paris, Texas* (1984); and almost everything by Theo Angelopoulos who, in complex works such as *Ulysses' Gaze* (1995), and *Eternity and a Day* (1998), creates complex temporal and spatial journeys through Greece and the Balkans as part of his obsessive exploration of issues of identity, memory and history, and the nature of border. For the purpose of this essay, however, I have chosen to concentrate primarily upon an Icelandic journey narrative or road movie: *Cold Fever*, directed by Fridrik Thor Fridriksson in 1994, not only because of the relative unfamiliarity of the setting, the stunning photography and the sensitive acting, but primarily because the film's playful narrative successfully foregrounds its self-conscious subversion of the Hollywood road movie genre, while seeming to comply fully with its dominant characteristics. And as we shall see, in this way the film explores not only issues of personal and national identity, but also the nature of European cinema itself.

Cold Fever as European Road Movie

Cold Fever, therefore, is a film that uses the physical and cultural displacement of exile to interrogate the complex nature of identity, particularly in relation to memory, language, and culture. The film's narrative trajectory is shaped by the bewildering and often dangerous journey across Iceland in midwinter, undertaken by Hirata Atsushi, a successful young Japanese business man who reluctantly finds himself obliged to perform certain traditional funeral rites at the remote river where his parents had perished in an accident some seven years previously. Abruptly transported from his safe and entirely predictable existence in Tokyo to the vast white unknown landscape of Iceland, Atsushi (following the route described by Rattle) moves from a secure, static, place-based definition of self, via alienation, insecurity, and the negotiation of difference, to a new personal geography or identity, based on movement and instability. His simultaneously spatial and physical journey across the capricious and dangerous landscape of Iceland, thus metaphorically depicts his inner journey to self-knowledge.

If we consider *Cold Fever* in terms of the four main criteria established by Corrigan in his study of the road movie genre, it is immediately clear that it offers a close degree of correlation. First of all, according to Corrigan, the road movie reflects the breakdown of the family unit, and articulates the destabilisation of male subjectivity and masculine empowerment. Its protagonist, he notes, is entirely at the mercy of the encounters and events that occur along the road, whilst his car itself acquires overwhelming importance as protection or promise of self and, in so doing, frequently assumes something of 'a human and spiritual reality'. And finally, the film's main focus is upon the male protagonist, within a form of escapist fantasy which relates masculinity to technology (Corrigan 1991: 143–46). In *Cold Fever*, Atsushi has indeed embarked upon his journey as a direct result of the disintegration of his family unit, following the untimely death of both his parents. Equally, by undermining the certainties which had previously defined his secure and static sense of self, Atsushi's journey makes him, perhaps for the first time ever, painfully aware of his own vulnerability. Moreover, we see that as Atsushi crosses the white expanse of Iceland, the car does increasingly function as his sole refuge, his only source of security or containment and that, in so doing, it often seems to assume a persona of its own. And although the journey is not initially perceived by Atsushi as a means of escape (unless from guilt, as he is made aware of his neglect of his parents while they were alive), it will ultimately enable him to escape into a new and open sense of selfhood.

Cold Fever also complies with the definitions of the road movie offered by Hayward: it is iconographically marked not only by road and car, but also by such elements as the tracking shot and wild open spaces; the journey narrative has a chronological structure, and its purpose is self-knowledge (Hayward 1996: 300–301). However, as I have intimated, whilst adopting the road movie format for his exploration of identity as process, Fridriksson constantly subverts it from within, and it is important to recognise and understand the significance of this as we explore the iconography of the road movie in relation to *Cold Fever*.

Home

As Robertson recognises, although the subject of the road movie is the journey, represented by the road, it remains nonetheless a genre 'obsessed with home'. In other words, the trope of the road depends upon home as a structuring absence (Robertson 1997: 271). Home thus emerges as the experienced norm, the place-based identity against which the encounters and vicissitudes of the journey will be measured. The opening sequence of *Cold Fever* clearly signifies home as locus of certainty and definition. The cinema screen itself is tightly constricted, its images confined to a small central area, surrounded by a wide frame of darkness. It is within this tightly confined space that we first encounter Atsushi, and we quickly understand that the thick black border which frames his screen image represents his subjective identity and viewpoint as much as his lifestyle; the persona he has so painstakingly constructed. As if to underline this point, Fridriksson creates ever tighter framings, ever more restricted enclosures within the narrow confines of this screen within a screen. For example, the tiny box-like room in which Atsushi lives, and where we first see him, is made tinier still by disturbingly low camera angles which emphasise its tall walls and claustrophobic dimensions. And within this confined box, our gaze, along with Atsushi's, is riveted on an even smaller box, the television, whose minute screen appears to constitute his narrow window on the world. The rigid spatial divisions of the screen indicate those that Atsushi has constructed within himself, so that even when he leaves his flat, on his way to work, there is no accompanying sense of freedom or release. The point becomes clear, if we make a direct comparison with, for example Truffaut's *Les 400 coups*

(France, 1959) in which the confined camera and rigidly compartmentalised interiors of home and school provide an
immediate and striking contrast with the open spaces and
mobile camera of the exterior shots, thus indicating that the
child at the centre of the story can indeed find freedom when
he escapes adult control. In these opening sequences of *Cold
Fever*, however, even when Atsushi leaves his flat, the screen
remains reduced, the camera retains its low angle, and the
shots are flattened, inevitably recalling Harvey's description of
film as 'a spectacle projected within an enclosed space on a
depthless screen' (Harvey 1989: 308). Atsushi's whole world,
therefore, is one of containment; a familiar, predictable, and
entirely enclosed space.

Atsushi's inner journey to self-knowledge begins as he
leaves the security of Japan for the unpredictability of Iceland.
As we have seen, he embarks upon this trip without enthusiasm; it is, after all, a far cry from the tightly organised golfing
holiday in Hawaii that he had planned, and his continuing
resistance to the journey is signified inside the aeroplane by a
further series of rigid framings. For example, his seat belt holds
him physically, while mentally he is absorbed in the tiny
screen of his laptop, unwilling to look out of the window at the
vast expanse of sky. However, when the chatty Icelandic
woman sitting next to him forces him to raise his eyes from
his computer, as she informs him that he will certainly love
Iceland, because everyone does, Atsushi's safe world is sud-
denly and irrevocably shattered. For as the woman speaks, the
images suddenly explode, filling the entire screen and breaking free from the inner framing that previously contained
them. And that screen reveals, quite literally, space: first the
whiteness of the mountains below, and then a vast snowscape
without definition. The total openness that greets Atsushi's
arrival in Iceland, removing at one fell swoop all the familiar
contours of his existence, thus clearly indicates what his journey has in store. However, he remains reluctant to set off, and
as he leaves the airport and takes his first steps in this alien
world, Atsushi immediately positions himself on the comforting black and white lines of a pedestrian crossing, in a vain
attempt to reassert some sense of control. However, as he
quickly discovers, any such security is illusory, for in Iceland
nothing can be polarised into black and white; no definitions
are certain.

The journey has now begun; the quirky Icelandic road
movie is underway. It is, however, important to note that the

journey is also, perhaps even primarily, a cinematic journey, in that our understanding of Atsushi thus far has been created almost entirely through the self-conscious geometry of the screen. Thus, the white space that meets Atsushi's hostile gaze, is inevitably recognised by the spectator as the white space of the cinema screen itself. And as Atsushi's journey advances, so the shallow images and restricted camera movements that characterised the Tokyo sequences are replaced by sweeping panoramas, and an increasingly mobile camera.

The Road

As meeting place of space and time, the road functions as one of the key signifiers in the road movie, establishing both the film's specific narrative trajectory and an extended metaphor of discovery and invention. Leading the protagonist away from home and towards the unknown, the road, as representation of escape and freedom, is of course accorded a particular significance in American culture, where it reflects the mythology of the frontier: 'The road defines the space between town and country. It is an empty expanse, a *tabula rasa*, the last true frontier' (Dargis 1991: 14–18). Whilst the road undoubtedly serves to provide direction for Atsushi's journey in *Cold Fever*, even this fundamental marker is portrayed as erratic and problematical, repeatedly disappearing from sight under unstable layers of ice and snow. This feature is significant, of course, because it implies that Atsushi is denied even this most basic marker or guide on his journey to self knowledge, but at the same time, it should be recognised as an example of the methods playfully used by Fridriksson to subvert the very genre he appears to be using, and to introduce a 'European' ambiguity into the clear-cut parameters of its Hollywood counterpoint.

One of the characteristic shots featured in the road movie is the direct cut between map and the territory it represents, and in general, as Schaber comments, the two tend to be mutually somewhat elusive (Schaber 1997: 25). In *Cold Fever* too, there is a proliferation of such shots, as Atsushi desperately tries to establish some sort of rational control over the natural chaos of the Icelandic landscape.[1] His attempts, of course, prove futile; devoid of recognisable features, its unmarked whiteness makes any form of definition impossible. In his essay on the effect of the floods which struck Paris in January 1955, Barthes observes that the sheet of water which effaces all the familiar landmarks and with them, any hierarchy of functions, also removes any indications of direction, any possible sense of forward movement (Barthes 1993: 599–601), and this denial of spatial and temporal indicators is exactly the effect the Icelandic countryside exercises over Atsushi. The undifferentiated whiteness that surrounds Atsushi is thus the antithesis, and the ultimate denial, of the rigidly structured sense of identity that had previously been his.

The Car

Clearly, the car too functions as a key signifier in the road movie where, traditionally it represents a clear sense of male identity for the protagonist through its status as an object that combines technology and modernity. For Jeff Hearn, this sense of identity represents a modern form of masculinity, 'founded on speed and fragmentary, fleeting images' (Hearn 1992: 198). And it is important to note, in this context, that although time and space could, of course, be conquered faster and more efficiently in an aeroplane, the key difference is that, as the driver of a car (or motor bike) the protagonist is actually generating and controlling the speed, and it is this feature that, in Hark's terms, gives his journey its particular 'phallic frisson' (Hark 1997: 214). Much as he would enjoy the experience, however, it is unlikely that Atsushi could obtain such pleasure from *his* vehicle: an old, unpredictable, and unreliable Citroën DS. Of course, the DS is a car with a vast range of European cultural implications, not least its status as icon for young French film directors, such as Godard and Truffaut, at the forefront of the New Wave movement of the late 1950s.[2] And although at that period, the DS was indeed considered to be a technological miracle, a work of art, an icon of modernity, and was described by Barthes, for example, as the modern cultural equivalent of the great Gothic cathedrals (passionately constructed by unknown artists, and creating a sense of magic for the whole nation), it must be admitted that it is a far cry from the efficient, 'sexy' modern vehicle that Atsushi desires, and it is significant that when it breaks down, marooning him in the mountains, it is the intervention of an Icelandic fairy, rather than a garage mechanic, that gets it going, and saves his life (Barthes 1993: 655). The very car seems therefore to offer an ironic resistance to its traditional filmic status as symbol of

American culture, at least as defined by Baudrillard as 'space, speed, cinema, technology' (Baudrillard 1988: 100). Interestingly, in this context, Barthes identifies in the radical new design of the DS, a shift away from car as object of speed to something more spiritual; it is a car which, as it were, exercises a form of control over movement, and thus can be understood as the antithesis of its American counterpart. And in the case of Atsushi's DS, even the radio proves resistant to 'global' American values, imposing (since it is impossible to turn it off) a relentless accompaniment of Icelandic folk and pop music.[3]

Earlier, we noted that the white and featureless snowscapes which replace Atsushi's own neatly structured and clearly delineated topographies would also serve to draw attention to the whiteness of the screen, wiped clear of its normal and identifiable images. In his treatment of the car, Fridriksson similarly draws attention to the self-referentiality of the genre. In addition to its implicit references to French New Wave films, the car itself functions as cinema as it drives forwards, in a series of shots in which its windscreen becomes the wide screen of the cinema, advancing the filmic narrative and alternating with the reflective and retrospective viewpoint provided by the smaller 'screen' of the rear mirror. Fridriksson's choice of a DS serves to highlight this function, for its huge windows, seen by Barthes as offering great expanses of air and nothingness, attract the eye and the camera in a self-conscious manner (Barthes 1993: 656). Thus the car provides a dual mise-en-abyme within the narrative, again drawing attention to the self-reflexivity of the genre as used by Fridriksson. As far as Atsushi is concerned, however, the car signifies security, as well as the possibility of journey, and the camera repeatedly cuts from panoramic travelling shots in which the car is the only distinguishable feature in the vast whiteness of the screen, to close-ups of Atsushi, huddled inside its protective shell. Essentially, it is these two aspects, its complex self-reflexivity, and its ability to represent simultaneous stasis and movement, that make the road movie such a powerful modernist form, as well, of course, as an effective metaphor for someone who, like Atsushi, is riding on the very edge of self-identity. In other words, the vehicle functions as a panoptic cell that offers the subject stasis, in contrast to the open-ended mobility of the road, as 'linear conduit to infinity' (Barthes 1993: 790–92, Aitken and Lukinbeal 1997: 349)

However, the DS constantly rejects this role, and seems to have an entirely different agenda. Being both perverse and unreliable, it has punctures, breaks down, and needs petrol, and ultimately, it is also unfaithful, abandoning Atsushi, and going off with someone else. Instead of protecting Atsushi from the vicissitudes of the journey, therefore, it repeatedly forces him to deal directly with the problems and differences he encounters. Given that awareness of self is predicated upon awareness of the other, such confrontations are, of course, essential to his development. As we remarked earlier, within the confines of home, Atsushi's only encounter with anything foreign had occurred via his television screen, primarily in the form of gameshows which, by ridiculing non-Japanese cultures contained them, rendering them unreal and un-threatening. In Iceland, however, the other is proximate at all times: Atsushi is obliged to speak a foreign language if he is to communicate, and to eat alien food, if he is to survive. And not only does the culture of Iceland, like its landscape, per-sistently refute the certainties upon which his earlier existence was predicated, but it also forces him to accept his own marginality; to recognise, in other words, that centre and periphery are relative and unstable concepts.

The film charts these invisible inner changes through a number of potent visual clues: for instance, the forms of trans-port used by Atsushi occur in a particular sequence: plane, bus, taxi, car, horse, foot, in recognition of the fact that he is assuming increasing personal responsibility for his journey. Furthermore, we might also see in this deliberate contrasting of passive and active travel Fridriksson's comparison of the discourses of Hollywood and of European cinema, in relation to the role of the spectator. And before such ideas are dis-missed as altogether too fanciful, I should like to point out the compelling evidence that results from the fact that embedded in the overall road movie structure, which I have posited as a European contextualisation of an American genre, we sud-denly find a 'real', Hollywood, road movie. The sequence in question, which lasts for a mere eleven minutes, occurs some two-thirds of the way into the film, and it might be tempting to see it as a near irrelevancy, a moment of light relief, albeit with sinister undertones, were it not that its clear status as a mise-en-abyme signals its key significance within the film. Not only does it constitute a turning point in Atsushi's journey to self-knowledge, signalling the moment at which he assumes an active responsibility for his quest, but it also enables Fridriksson to provide a specific contrast between the identities of Icelandic/European cinema and popular culture with those of America, as well as foregrounding, for the spectator, the self-conscious modernist relationship between narrative as journey (road), and image production (film) that we noted earlier.

Hollywood and Iceland: Road Movie at the Crossroads

The sequence in question begins as Atsushi stops to pick up a pair of hitchhikers who appear, as if from nowhere, in the snowy landscape. In so doing, he unwittingly allows his own road movie to be hijacked by an American road movie of the Bonnie and Clyde sub-genre, with its own very different agenda. Whilst the couple introduce themselves as Jack and Jill, tourists 'from the US of A', it is apparent (to us, if not to Atsushi), that their names are false, and that this is a typical road movie couple, fleeing from the law. Moreover, picked as it were out of the blue, the choice of Jack must inevitable carry with it references to Jack Kerouac, whose novel *On the Road*, published in 1959, had a seminal influence on the development of the road movie genre.

On Jack and Jill's terms, the incident is entirely successful. They acquire the fast food and Diet Pepsi they crave. Jack shoots a young Icelandic girl as part of his robbery of a small roadside shop, before successfully transforming the stately DS into an unlikely get-away car (a 'gun on wheels'). And finally they steal the car at gunpoint, abandoning Atsushi to the snow. During the sequence the cutting speeds up somewhat, and there are moments of tension based on sex, pornography, and violence which are entirely absent elsewhere in the film. However, Fridriksson's playful and ironic treatment makes it impossible for us to view the sequence on Jack and Jill's terms. For a start, the couple are as ridiculous as they are sinister: argumentative, chauvinistic, and unstable, they repeatedly insult Atsushi and Japanese culture ('Guess you Japs must be everywhere'; 'Let's go, Chinaman'); Icelandic culture (describing the car as an 'Icelandic torture chamber' because of the music on the 'stupid Nazzi radio'), and each other. Jack trots out inevitable clichés about the space and freedom of being on the road ('God's country'), as he stands urinating in the snow, and he is rude and abusive towards the young Icelandic girl in the shop, forcing her to look at pornographic images, before masturbating in the lavatory over the dirty magazine he has pinched, or so we assume; for within Hollywood conventions, such an act could never directly be shown. Indeed, it seems that Fridriksson here is deliberately targeting the stringent rules imposed by Hollywood in relation to the representation of sex in couple-based road movies, and the deferral strategies and fetishistic devices which result. Thus, he depicts Jack and Jill as a couple who are able to find gratification only through violence, and can communicate with each other only through their childish play with glove puppets.[4] As we have seen, Fridriksson's ironic gaze prevents us from taking the pair too seriously, and when they steal Atsushi's car, leaving him to continue on foot through the ice and snow, it is they who become irrelevant, driving out of the film, whilst our gaze, with that of the camera, remains fixed upon Atsushi. Nevertheless, they serve to perform a number of vital functions within the narrative. Firstly, they force Atsushi to recognise his own (Japanese) marginality to both sides of the European /American divide, thus further destabilising his earlier secure and static concept of identity. Secondly, by ejecting him entirely from the relative protection provided by the car, they force him to assume a positive and active role within the process of journey: he refuses to deviate from his objective, even when threatened with death, and from this point onwards, he will (at least for the most part), travel on horse back or on foot, no longer isolated from the land through which he is moving. Finally, by depositing Atsushi at an (unsignposted) crossroads, with its visual dialectic of centre and periphery, margin and mainstream, Fridriksson draws us, the spectators, directly into the process of reassessment the film articulates.

Icelandic Cowboys

Having, as it were, 'disposed' of Hollywood, by showing the ultimate irrelevance of Jack and Jill, Fridriksson cannot resist a further playful dig. As Atsushi continues his journey on foot, inadequately dressed, and still gripping his laptop, his next bizarre encounter will again juxtapose America and Europe, this time, in relation to the Western. Entering a small bar/hotel in the first village he reaches, a bewildered Atsushi finds that he has arrived at the home of Icelandic cowboys, just in time for their special festival. Our initial reaction might be that Fridriksson is pointing out the hijacking of Icelandic culture by that of America, that he is observing the process of globalisation that is so confidently predicted. However, it rapidly becomes clear that the Icelanders have not merely subverted the cowboy genre, but have entirely claimed it as their own, as their particularly Icelandic celebrations reveal. Not only do Icelandic cowboys have sheep instead of cows, but the whole tenor of their cowboy festival is entirely Icelandic: competitions to decide the best ram; culinary specialities such as sheeps' heads and rams' balls, washed down with the national drink, aptly known as Black Death; increasingly drunken renderings of Icelandic ballads and dances. It may indeed be the case, as Sorlin suggests, that we Europeans 'create and imagine the world through Hollywood's lenses', but as Fridriksson persuasively reveals, the images we project are stubbornly and self-consciously our own (Sorlin 1991: 1).

The role of the Icelandic cowboy interlude within Atsushi's own road movie, is to plunge him entirely into the Icelandic culture he has previously attempted to keep at a distance. We see him quite literally drinking in that culture, and as he becomes increasingly inebriated and relaxed during the course of the long evening, he forms a friendship with an elderly man who will act as guide and mentor on the final stage of his spiritual and physical journey. Watching their friendship develop, we see how Atsushi's previously closed and compartmentalised mind becomes increasingly receptive and open to dreams, stories, and myths that before then would have been dismissed by him as irrelevant superstition. Through this new openness, and through his attempts to share languages and traditions with his new friend instead of seeing them as boundary markers signifying difference, Atsushi begins to be aware of the qualities that actually link the physical and mental topographies of Japan and Iceland. In other words, the inner boundaries which initially served to define his identity no longer exist, and the new openness and receptivity which result have, in fact, been brought about through the process of journey. Thus the road movie has carried Atsushi from home to homelessness, from closure to openness, from certainty to insecurity. The letter he writes to his Grandfather, and which we hear in voice-over at the end of the film, just after he has completed his funeral rites, confirms this. He has learned, he says, that the journeys that really matter are those that cannot be described or defined; that are unmappable. By this stage, he has also realised that it is the travelling, rather than the destination, that counts, since identity is open-ended and mobile; a process, not a state. The perceived end of Atsushi's road movie is thus only the beginning, for there can be no ultimate closure.

The Open-Ended Destinations of Journey

Ever since Lumière's pioneering study of a train pulling into the station at La Ciotat, in the south of France (1895), film narratives have been obsessed with the theme of journey. And whether such journey narratives echo the frontier mythology of the United States, or European experiences of emigration, exile, and exclusion, it is clear that they play a key role in both reflecting and making sense of these experiences, as well as providing a potent means of articulating and exploring the fluid identities of the late twentieth century.

Writing about the Swiss director, Alain Tanner, Lieve Spaas describes his short experimental video film, *Temps mort* (1978) (made by attaching a video camera onto the window of his car), as 'a real "journey film", where the camera itself becomes the traveller', and she comments that this experiment 'elicits a comparison between film-making and travelling' (Spaas 2000: 161). While this observation is, of course true, we might equally claim that what Tanner is actually doing is making explicit the mechanics of film itself: the camera's shifting viewpoint, allied with the dynamic juxtaposition of images through editing, inevitably establishes film narrative as a spatio-temporal journey which perpetually repositions its spectators, drawing them directly into 'an active collaboration with the dynamic technical relations and motions of modern culture' (Roberts 1998: 20–21). Film does not posit identity as static or fixed, so much as a constant state of movement and insecurity, for its moving images inevitably deconstruct the present, even as they create it. It can thus be seen to articulate the fundamentally 'discontinuous state of being' which is one of Edward Saïd's definitions of exile (Saïd 2001: 177). And if for Steiner it appears entirely fitting that 'those who create art in a civilisation of quasi-barbarism, which has made so many homeless, should themselves be *poets unhoused and wanderers across language*' (quoted in Saïd, 2001: 174 (my italics)), then it is amongst such artists that we must situate contemporary European film directors, themselves perpetual wanderers across the visual landscapes of images.

Theo Angelopoulos, who sees all his films as ongoing journeys in which 'the hero's homecoming is also a departure, the beginning of a new journey', defines his notion of home as 'a car passing through a landscape' (Angelopoulos in Fainaru 2001: 90). These comments, which neatly recall both Tanner's experimental film and the journey narrative of *Cold Fever*, can equally serve to provide a more general view of contemporary film.

In this brief and necessarily partial account, I have attempted to indicate a number of ways in which, by subverting the road movie genre from within, Fridriksson is able to extend the narrative layers of *Cold Fever* to include a study of the identity of contemporary European cinema and its uneasy relationship with Hollywood as Other. And it is clear that, in so doing, he formulates an upbeat and positive prognosis for its survival. But it is above all essential to be aware of what such journey narratives indicate about contemporary identities, and of their fundamental recognition that, as the main character in *The Suspended Step of the Stork* (Angelopoulos, 1991) comments, 'being a refugee is an *internal* condition more than an external one'.

Notes

1. We may also recognise here a further reference to the essential modernism of the road movie genre, as Atsushi's attempt to order space rationally can be directly equated with Harvey's identification of accurate maps and chronometers as essential tools of modernism (Harvey 1989: 249).
2. When spoken, its very name underlines the car's iconic status since phonetically, 'DS' exactly replicates 'Déesse', the French word for Goddess.
3. Fridriksson might well be making a direct reference to the representation of American culture in other European road movies such as *Alice in the Cities* (Wim Wenders, 1974), whose narrative is pervaded by the bland American pop music churned out by the car radio.
4. It would seem reasonable to suggest that the characters of Jack and Jill are here being exposed as mere puppets in the Hollywood system because they are obliged to conform to its conventions, whereas Atsushi, and Fridriksson, are actively subversive in their treatment of the genre.

References

Aitken, S. and C. Lukinbeal (1997) 'Disassociated Masculinities and Geographies of the Road', in Cohan, S. and I. R. Hark (eds), *The Road Movie Book*, London and New York: Routledge, 349–70.

Barthes, R. (1993) *Oeuvres complètes*, vol. 1, Paris: Editions du Seuil.

Baudrillard, J. (1988) *America*, translated by C. Turner, London:
Verso.

Cohan, S. and I. R. Hark (1997) *The Road Movie Book*, London and
New York: Routledge.

Corrigan, T. (1991) *A Cinema Without Walls: Movies and Culture after
Vietnam*, New Brunswick, New Jersey: Rutgers University Press.

Dargis, M. (1991) 'Roads to freedom', *Sight and Sound* 3, 14–18.

Deleuze, G. (1986) *Cinema 1: the Movement-Image*, London: Athlone,
3–24.

Fainaru, D. (ed.), (2001) *Theo Angelopoulos Interviews*, Jackson:
University Press of Mississippi.

Hall, M. (1996) *Leaving Home. A conducted tour of twentieth-century
music with Simon Rattle*, London: Faber and Faber.

Hark, I. R. (1997) 'Fear of Flying: Yuppie critique and the
buddie-road movie in the 1980s', in Cohan, S. and I. R. Hark
(eds), *The Road Movie Book*, London and New York: Routledge,
204–229.

Harvey, D. (1989) *The Condition of Postmodernity*, Cambridge, Mass.
and Oxford: Blackwell.

Hayward, S. (1996) *Key concepts in cinema studies*, London and New
York: Routledge.

Hearn, G. (1992) *Men in the Public Eye: The Construction and Deconstruction of Public Men and Public Patriarchies*, London: Routledge.

Jesinghausen, M. (2000) 'The Sky over Berlin as Transcendental
Space: Wenders, Doblin and the "Angel of History", in
Konstantarakos, M. (ed.) *Spaces in European Cinema*, Exeter and
Portland, OR.: Intellect, 77–92.

Roberts, J. (1998) *The art of interruption: Realism, photography and the
everyday*, Manchester and New York: Manchester University Press.

Robertson, P. (1997) 'Home and Away: Friends of Dorothy on the
road in Oz', in Cohan, S. and I. R. Hart (eds), *The Road Movie
Book*, London and New York: Routledge, 271–86.

Saïd, E. W. (2001) *Reflections on Exile and Other Literary and Cultural
Essays*, London: Granta Books.

Schaber, B. (1997) '"Hitler can't keep them that long": The road, the
people', in Cohan, S. and I. R. Hart (eds), *The Road Movie Book*,
London and New York: Routledge, 17–44.

Sorlin, P. (1991) *European Cinemas, European Societies 1939–1990*,
London and New York: Routledge.

Spaas, L. (2000) 'Centre, Periphery and Marginality in the Films of
Alain Tanner, in Konstantarakos, M. (ed.), *Spaces in European
Cinema*, Exeter and Portland, OR.: Intellect, 152–65.

CHAPTER 3

THE EXILE OF REMEMBERING: MOVEMENT AND MEMORY IN CHRIS MARKER'S *SANS SOLEIL*

Catherine Lupton

Traveller's Tales

He described me his reunion with Tokyo, like a cat who's come home from vacation in his basket immediately starts to inspect familiar places. He ran off to see if everything was where it should be: the Ginza owl, the Shimbashi locomotive, the temple of the fox at the top of the Mitsukoshi department store, which he found invaded by little girls and rock singers. He was told that it was now little girls who made and unmade stars, that producers shuddered before them …. Everything interested him. He who didn't give a damn if the Dodgers won the pennant or about the results of the Daily Double, asked feverishly how Chiyonofuji had done in the last sumo tournament. He asked for news of the imperial family, the crown prince, of the oldest mobster in Tokyo who appears regularly on television to teach goodness to children. These simple joys he had never felt of returning to a country, a house, a family home. But 12 million anonymous inhabitants could supply him with them.[1]

This passage from the voice-over commentary of Chris Marker's *Sans Soleil* [*Sunless*] (1982), accompanies a deft montage sequence of sights and scenes on the streets of Tokyo, shot with the familiar hand-held immediacy of the observational documentary style. At the beginning of the sequence, commentary and images lock neatly together: everything is indeed where it should be. Footage of motor expressways taken from inside a moving vehicle corroborates the account of the traveller's return; we are then shown the owl, the locomotive and the temple as each in turn is named. From this point on, narration and images drift apart. Each provides its own distinct itinerary of the rediscovered city, and to the extent that the two accounts hold together, it is by subliminal affinity rather than descriptive anchorage. The mention of the philanthropic mobster is made over a shot of a cat peering over a parapet, then a swift pan to the sign of the Hotel Utopia. Eventually the spoken track falls silent and allows the swift succession of snapshot-like images to flow on without comment, suggesting perhaps only what the voice-over had earlier reported about our traveller's singular obsession with banality: 'I've been round the world several times and now only banality still interests me. On this trip, I've tracked it with the relentlessness of a bounty hunter.'

This sequence serves effectively to introduce a familiar view of Chris Marker as the inveterate globetrotter, the mobile image scavenger who displaces and mediates his own experiences of travel via a palimpsest of imaginary alter egos. The commentary of *Sans Soleil* takes the form of letters sent by a fictional cameraman, Sandor Krasna, to an unseen woman who reads them out and comments upon them. We only discover Krasna's identity in the closing credits: the voice of the film speaks anonymously and refers to her correspondent only as 'he'. The information and opinions we hear expressed in the voice-over are filtered through hearsay, reported speech and secondary interpretation. In the passage just referred to, the woman's voice is heard glossing Krasna's account of his travels and expressing opinions about his behaviour. Some of the information relayed from Krasna is dependent upon what others have told him; such as what we learn about the power that the little girls wield over the commercial fortunes of the rock singers. As the film proceeds, we discover that Krasna is given to quoting from the writings, letters and sayings of others: the poet Bashō, the revolutionaries Amilcar Cabral and Miguel Torga, the kamikaze pilot Ryoji Uebara, Marlon Brando in the role of Colonel Kurtz in *Apocalypse Now*, and so on.

Krasna's reported sentiments upon his return to Tokyo exhibit the enviable knack of being completely at home in a foreign country, of finding a niche on bustling city streets and greater kinship with twelve million strangers than with the ideals of national belonging, home and family, which we are told hold no attraction for him. This habit of locating the domestic within the exotic, of pointing to the familiar within the strange, is a defining trait of Marker's earlier, celebrated travel-essay-films made in the second half of the 1950s. At the close of *Dimanche à Pékin* [*A Sunday in Peking*] (1955) – whose title itself fuses the faraway destination with the routine ritual of the weekend outing – the voice-over narration reflects upon a river scene by the Summer Palace, saying 'All of this is far away like China, and at the same time as familiar as the Bois de Boulogne or the banks of the Loing'.[2] *Lettre de Sibérie* [*Letter from Siberia*] (1958), opens with a quotation from Henri Michaux's *Lointain intérieur* – the line 'I am writing to you from a far country' – which pitches the intimate address of the epistolatory voice within the distant, enigmatic world of Siberia; and shortly afterwards observes of the rolling, verdant landscape on screen that it might be Ermenonville or New England, were it not for the distinctive dress of the man we then see working up a telegraph pole, and the fact that the other end of the telegraph line is eight thousand kilometres away. If *Dimanche à Pékin* presumes France to be the projected homeland, *Lettre de Sibérie* offers a choice – it could be France or the United States – which interestingly prefigures the way that, in the sequence describing Krasna's return to Tokyo, the different language versions of *Sans Soleil* name different things to convey a sense of home and national belonging. In the English version quoted above, the cultural reference points are American. In the French language version of the same passage, the equivalents are a goal by the French soccer star Michel Platigny and a win on the *tiercé* – France's system for betting on horseracing.[3] The choices are tailored to resonate with the film's presumed audience, rather than establishing a fixed national identity for Sandor Krasna.

Room to Roam

The recurrence within Chris Marker's work of the imagined traveller who can find home wherever they find themselves, appears on first inspection less to fit the profile of the exile than that of the nomad. In an essay entitled 'Exile, Nomadism and Diaspora: the Stakes of Mobility in the Western Canon', John Durham Peters establishes the following definitions of the three terms (Peters 1999: 17–37). The exile is traditionally one banished from home and unable to return, so the idea of a fixed home assumes tremendous importance within exilic discourse as the lost centre that becomes the focus of nostalgic, compensatory projections of former stability, coherence and happiness. Durham Peters explores a range of instances where theological and philosophical usage has gradually reinterpreted the concept of exile as a more generalised spiritual or existential state of incompletion, and in the process made it more of a 'mission' than a 'punishment' – a line of thinking that finds affinity with more recent studies of the positive and creative aspects of exile cultures (see Naficy 1993). Fundamentally, though, exile remains dependent upon the sense of home being 'elsewhere' and inaccessible. The second term, diaspora, shares with exile the movement away from an original homeland, but places more emphasis upon the creation of networks and relationships among the dispersed community. Durham Peters characterises exile as a melancholy and solitary state; diaspora as adaptive, communicative and collective. Finally, the nomad dispenses altogether with attachment to a home fixed in space and time, and instead takes their home with them wherever they go. The modern idea of nomadism, which goes beyond describing actual nomadic peoples to suggest an attitude of mind which anyone can practise, was first developed by the American philosopher Ralph Waldo Emerson in his 1841 essay 'History'. Emerson defined nomadism as the 'faculty of rapid domestication', which allows an individual to find 'points of interest wherever fresh objects meet his eyes' (quoted in Peters 1999: 30). The qualities Emerson associates with nomadism are rapid and positive adaptation to new circumstances and surroundings, and the capacity to constantly find new sources of interest and wonder, this latter faculty embracing not only the appreciation of new places, but also the ability to perceive familiar environments as novel and strange.

The enthusiasm with which Chris Marker's imagined protagonists encounter and record new territories, and effortlessly find analogies that communicate the sense of being temporarily at home there, carries clear echoes of Emerson's nomadism, as succinctly expressed by his follower David Thoreau: 'the art is to travel without ever leaving home'. A broader survey of the content and formal strategies of *Sans Soleil* discovers further evidence for considering it a nomadic text. Two features of the film are worth singling out: perpetual travel as its ruling motif, and its intricate play of constructed and borrowed identities: the philosophical condition of post-structural, postmodern subjectivity which John Durham Peters associates explicitly with nomadism (Peters 1999: 31–32).

Few films 'roam through all the latitudes' (Emerson, quoted in Peters 1999: 34) with the breathless mobility of *Sans Soleil*. The film touches down in Japan, Okinawa, Guinea-Bissau, the Cape Verde Islands, Iceland, San Francisco and the Ile-de-France. Borrowed film extracts transport us further: to the African savannah, to Portugal. At one point we are told that we are near the Dutch border, at another we see a satellite in space and a Polaris missile being launched over the ocean. This potent sense of perpetual geographical displacement is underscored by the incessant and varied representation of means of transport: trains, aeroplanes, road vehicles, ferries, canoes; seen from both inside and outside. The voice-over recounts actual journeys, imagined journeys, voyages in space, time, fantasy and dream, and journeys that cannot take place. People are shown on a jetty in the Cape Verde Islands: how long, wonders the commentary, have they been waiting there for the ferry to arrive?

The prevailing impression of mobility, of the lack of a stable resting place, permeates *Sans Soleil* beyond its overt represen-tations of travel. The pace of the montage is hectic: a typical experience reported by viewers is the inability to grasp the film, certainly the first time they see it and often after subse-quent viewings, the feeling that it speeds past and slips away beyond reach, generating the need to watch it again.[4] The content of the images that pass by so swiftly is marked by tran-sience, the sense of time passing (see Russell 1999: 304). People constantly move through and beyond the frame, the sun sets, rain falls, things decay or are destroyed. Images depicting con-ventional domestic spaces – homes, private interiors, personal belongings, any sense of enclosure, ownership and rootedness – are extremely rare in *Sans Soleil*. The film is dominated by the non-place and the public space: stations, ports, ferries, trains, city streets, department stores, parks, concourses, showrooms, bars, markets, hotels, temples, cemeteries, and museums. Vast, empty landscapes – deserts, the volcanic lunar terrain of Ice-land, stretches of verdant countryside – counterpoint the rep-resentation of the bustling urban world, but these are equally undomesticated realms with few signs of human presence and habitation. *Sans Soleil* does make frequent use of close-ups to pick individuals out of the crowds and observe them, but they are represented as belonging and being themselves through collective, public activities: rituals, ceremonies, celebrations and routine daily actions. *Sans Soleil* invites us to consider the idea that what we are accustomed to think of as collective values and sentiments are only an accumulation of private interests, longings or disappointments: 'men ... parade their personal laceration in the great wound of history'.

Le Voyageur sans bagages

As mentioned earlier, John Durham Peters observes an analogy between nomadism and the constructed identity formations of postmodern and post-structural philosophy: the notion that the self is not essential and fixed but perpetually in process, not self-generating but 'always-already' written by pre-existing cultural and social practices, in relation to which subjectivity operates in open-ended dynamic tension. *Sans Soleil* could be read as an exemplary text of this postmodern selfhood, with its endlessly multiplied voices and personae, its fondness for verbal and visual quotation,[5] and its refusal to anchor being and identity in visible bodies and defined characters. Rather like the vivid cosmic image of the universe as having its centre everywhere and its circumference nowhere, the experience of a self addressing us in *Sans Soleil* is intimate and immediate, but it is impossible to delimit that self: to discern its origins or its destination, to confine it within the boundaries of a specific and discrete individual.

Contrary to this principle of limitless and multiple subjectivity in *Sans Soleil*, a number of writers have sought to manage its exhaustive complexity by reading its meanings back onto its author, Chris Marker. Catherine Russell and John Welchman offer readings of *Sans Soleil* which posit Marker as the stable and privileged auteur, whose projection of multiple alter egos and subject-positions is so much dissimulation: the dubious concealment of a fixed and assured identity that does not want to expose itself to critical scrutiny (see Welchman 1996: 336–50, Russell 1999: 301–11). Welchman writes of the 'ineffable origins and unflappable presents' of the 'dispersed personae' in Marker's films, concluding that Marker 'simultaneously surrenders to the poetry of the other place, and reins himself back with an intrusive, confessional, believable, diary-documentary voice. As a result, his pieces are strangely, pleasurably but also easily sutured, joining together the imagining of intangible others and the Fantastic Travels of Mandeville, with a lyrical yet foot-firm, anecdotal, walk-and-talk-about I' (Welchman 1996: 348 and 349).

For Russell, Marker is a melancholy modernist, whose film does have the virtue of addressing the impossibility of his own perspective, as one absolutely detached by race, gender, education and privilege from the places and people he films and describes; but which can only reproduce the mechanisms of that detachment: what she regards as Marker's persistent severing of images from their own cultural, historical and political contexts, and his voyeuristic and fetishistic desire to possess images of his sexual and racial Other. 'In the labyrinth of reflecting mirrors, the dislocated global perspective ultimately points back to the subject position of the Western avant-garde filmmaker and his complicit audience' (Russell 1999: 305).

There is a significant correlation between these criticisms of *Sans Soleil*, and wider objections that have been levelled against contemporary nomadism. John Durham Peters surveys the arguments of nomadism's detractors, notably the close links that have been observed between the modern nomad and various forms of social privilege – based in race, class, gender, nationality and language. Not everyone has the resources or the freedom to wander at will, whether through intellectual enquiry or actual travel. Transient nomadic appropriation is also accused of objectifying, exoticising and then abandoning host cultures, trading in a spectacle of Otherness which avoids any genuine engagement with cultural and racial diversity (see Peters 1999: 34ff).

In contrast to the cautionary auteurist readings of *Sans Soleil*, Stella Bruzzi questions any straightforward identification of the film's voice with that of Chris Marker (Bruzzi 2000: 57–64). She focuses on the complex resonances of the female speaking voice used in the film, arguing that critics who insist that it is ultimately Marker who is talking to us, are striving to impose order and hierarchy on a text which is challenging precisely because the relationships between voice and image, and between the various narrative and narrating personae, are so fluid and impossible to pin down. She claims that '[w]hat characterises the female voice-over is the inconsistency of its reported relationship with Krasna' (Bruzzi 2000: 60–61), observing that, if at times the woman's voice seems to be merely a passive vehicle relaying the cameraman's thoughts and observations, when it shifts to commenting upon and interpreting Krasna's letters, the woman seems to express her own opinions and feelings. One effect of this implied gap between Krasna's 'voice' and the woman's, is that it allows the possibility of critical detachment from Krasna's ostensible control of the film's discourse. It is worth stressing that the meanings and origins of *Sans Soleil*'s commentary remain fundamentally elusive – one can rarely be certain how a particular phrase is meant to be interpreted, and who is the author of it. In the reunion with Tokyo sequence, the woman's recounting of Krasna's nomadic habits could equally be heard as admiration or gentle mockery – the listener is not obliged automatically to endorse his indifference to domestic rootedness, but is free to consider him from the viewpoint of one who does not share in this behaviour, whether through temperament or conviction.[6]

Journeying Backwards

Approximately two-thirds of the way through *Sans Soleil*, Krasna's wanderings take him to San Francisco, to tour the locations of Alfred Hitchcock's *Vertigo* (1958). His pilgrimage becomes the occasion for a re-telling of the narrative of *Vertigo*, as contemporary footage described as the record of Krasna's visit is intercut with (predominantly) still images from Hitchcock's film, but with a notable condensation and re-arrangement of events as they appear in the original plot. *Sans Soleil* ends its re-telling at the Golden Gate Bridge with Madeleine's (Kim Novak) attempted suicide, an event which occurs mid-way through the first half of Hitchcock's film, before what the *Sans Soleil* version has already revealed of the subsequent death of Madeleine, and Scottie's (James Stewart) attempt to recreate her by making over Judy (Kim Novak again), a woman he meets who bears an uncanny resemblance to Madeleine.

The replay of *Vertigo* is an extremely significant moment in *Sans Soleil*, because it marks the point at which its perpetual nomadic movement is unmasked and put into reverse. The meditation upon Hitchcock's film becomes testimony to a counter-nomadic impulse in Marker's: the desire not to move incessantly forwards but to go back, to return to a moment in the past which has been irrevocably lost, but which continues to exert an irresistible imaginative lure upon the subject. The impulse, in short, of the exile. The commentary prefigures this reversal by obliquely acknowledging the film's blithe meandering as a form of frantic self-protection: 'Memories must make do with their delirium, with their drift. A moment stopped would burn like a frame of film blocked before the furnace of the projector.' This admission heralds the surrender to the obsessive, exilic logic of *Vertigo*, a film whose dominant theme is mirrored in John Durham Peters's definition of the psychoanalytic concept of exile as 'the fact that time, by destroying the objects of our love, makes a desire for return (that is, repetition compulsion) a structural element of the human psyche' (Peters 1999: 21). The compulsion to repeat *Vertigo* in *Sans Soleil* plays out as multiple viewing (Krasna has seen the film nineteen times), the obsessive attention to the details of the location sites, and the formal use of still frames from Hitchcock's film that are held for a few moments and then dissolved, mimicking the freezing and obliteration of blocked memories.

Krasna admires *Vertigo* as the only film, in his opinion, to have portrayed 'impossible memory, insane memory'. Memory is impossible because it annihilates time, and by extension annihilates the subject who exists in time and remembers. In *Vertigo*, Scottie's drive to recreate Madeleine and to piece together the events leading up to her death, brings him ultimately to the dreadful realisation that Madeleine was already Judy, and that in remodelling Judy as Madeleine, he was merely repeating what another man had already done. Scottie is doomed to complete the circle and to watch Madeleine die a second time. In the final shot of *Vertigo* he stands on the parapet of the church tower looking down at her body, in the same crooked posture that he had when he dreamed of his own body falling in Madeleine's place.

Marker had paid homage to *Vertigo* before, in *La Jetée* (1962), the science fiction fable of a man imprisoned in subterranean Paris, after the city has been destroyed by the Third World War, who is used for time-travel experiments because he is so strongly marked by a memory from his childhood. When the experiments are completed, he is offered the chance to live in the future, a time when human functions have been perfected, including memory and the capacity to move in time at will. But the man chooses instead to return to the moment of his childhood memory, hoping to rejoin the woman he had met on his journeys into the past, only to discover that what he remembered so vividly was the moment of his own death. *Sans Soleil* recalls *La Jetée* as the 'other film' in which, like *Vertigo*, hands point at the rings in a slice of sequoia trunk. *La Jetée* was also composed, like elements of the *Vertigo* replay, (almost) entirely from still images with a separate voice-over narration.

In the sequence that immediately follows the *Vertigo* tour in *Sans Soleil*, we learn about an idea for a science fiction film that Sandor Krasna would like to make. It concerns a time traveller from the year 4001, the age of mental perfection and total memory recall, who becomes fascinated by the emotional resonance of memory in his planet's imperfect past, when memories meant something because so much else was forgotten. This hypothetical film can be read as reworking the outcome of *La Jetée*,[7] as if that film's hero had chosen the future instead of the past, and then regretted it. It is telling that in both cases the impulse to return is thwarted: the hero of *La Jetée* dies, and we hear that Krasna will never get round to making his film, which would have been called *Sans Soleil*.

Memory in *Sans Soleil* is a nomadic line of flight that runs back upon itself, but has to keep moving because it cannot really return: 'the eternal magnetic tape of a time that has to re-read itself constantly in order to know that it existed.' The exhilaration of travel and perpetual motion, the capacity to be 'homeless and home-ful' (Peters 1999: 21) at the same time, seem to indicate a desire to escape exilic longing for the past, to inhabit a realm of 'memories whose only function had been to leave behind nothing but memories.' This impulse certainly seems to account for Krasna's fascination with Japan, which at one point he describes as 'a world of appearances', in which memory is 'an impossibility'. But such a desire is its own undoing: memories are by nature the site of irreparable loss, they have no identity or meaning except in relation to forgetting and obliteration. This is why the 'image of happiness' that opens *Sans Soleil* – the three blond children walking on a sunny road in Iceland in 1965 – cannot find its place, except in the context of the volcanic eruption that destroyed the world they lived in. The image is archetypally idyllic, connoting a state of primordial innocence, the Eden before the Fall which is also alluded to in the commentary as we watch images of copulating stuffed animals in the Josankei sex museum, and which recalls theological interpretations of exile as a state of being cast out from spiritual wholeness or grace. But until the shot of the children is framed against other images that depict the erasure of the world it belonged to, it makes no sense. We learn that Krasna cannot make it work with other images, so it has to be isolated at the beginning of the film, by a material portent of its eventual right place (the 'long piece of black leader' that we watch and are told about), until the point is reached when it can be woven into the film's fabric of remembrance and annihilation.

Exile Images

In *Sans Soleil* the memory image functions to shield the subject from loss, from the unthinkable and the unrepresentable. The film expresses a desire for images that are no longer strictly speaking representations, images that do not mediate or translate, that carry no reminder of the erased contexts that produced them. We watch limpid scenes of Tokyo's streets and temples in January, and listen to the report of Krasna's reverie: 'I remember that month of January in Tokyo, or rather I remember the images that I filmed in that month of January in Tokyo. They have substituted themselves for my memory – they are my memory'. But at the same time such poignant images have their source in loss, the unthinkable and the unrepresentable, and can do nothing but point inexorably back to them. The question 'How can one remember thirst?' which occurs near the beginning of *Sans Soleil*, over a stilled frame of an African woman in a boat who is staring into the camera, both conveys the unrepresentability of thirst, and irresistibly prompts the viewer to try to recollect or imagine it. Memory images reveal and conceal in the same moment, they protect and expose.

These qualities of the memory image in *Sans Soleil* have considerable affinity with Homi Bhaba's conception of an exilic optic (Bhaba 1999: viii–xi). Bhaba refers to the contemporary media landscape and its characteristic features of acceleration and displacement: the increasing speed of modern communications networks, and their continual movement towards new representations (both of which have been noted as key elements of *Sans Soleil*). He argues that these qualities have the capacity to unsettle the stable habit of national identity, by carrying intimations of the political, social and economic dependence of fixed patterns of national being and belonging upon the forcible displacement (or exiling) of others. What interests Bhaba is the possibility of an exilic optic – in his account a way of seeing rather than a specific type of image – that can grasp the manifest content of a media representation, and simultaneously intuit what is exiled from that representation, which for Bhaba is both social and psychic repressed knowledge. The exilic optic avoids manifesting and defining this repressed knowledge as the 'negative' of the image, thereby containing it as one half of a stable binary opposition.

> But this is not a 'void' that becomes the ontological center for a simply 'negative', or negating, glance. It is by way of the process of erasure-within-exposure that a certain media temporality – 'a tiny spark of contingency' – shuttles in an exilic movement to make *at once* contiguous, and *in that flash*, contingent, the realms of human consciousness and the unconscious, the discourses of history and psychoanalysis. It is this juxtapositional movement that I want to describe as the inscription of an exilic optic (Bhaba 1999: xi)

Sans Soleil may be regarded as a film that constantly proffers its own images to be viewed through the oblique lens of Bhaba's exilic optic. The separation of the voice-over from the images, and the pervasive uncertainty about their precise relationship to each other, play a crucial role in this respect. The perpetual shocks and displacements of the montage do some of the work of unveiling otherness within the memory image, but it is the commentary that persistently hints at what lies on its far side: loss, destruction, death, horror, the brutal ruptures of history, abandonment, the unrepresentable, the unconscious. These are things we cannot literally see and contain because they are necessarily absent from the protective realm of the memory image, but they are still there, hovering at the limit of recognition, just beyond the borders of its frame. We are informed that we must learn to confront horror, to make a friend of it, as Colonel Kurtz says in *Apocalypse Now*, by recognising that it has 'a name and a face'. But all *Sans Soleil* actually offers is an infinite series of substitutes: each time 'another name and another face' arises to shield the subject from absolute horror, and to open towards it.

The Wounds of History

Sans Soleil tries to find a solution to the fearful instability of the memory image in the virtual world of the Zone, the digital image synthesiser owned by Krasna's friend Hayao Yamaneko. Changing the images of the past, transforming them from mimetic, photographic representations into vivid, shifting fields of flat, pixellated colour, is a way of making images bear the marks of degradation and loss inflicted by the passage of time.[8] Catherine Russell approaches the Zone as a mechanism which cuts Marker off from history, allowing images to be removed from their historical, social and cultural contexts; pinned down, manipulated and eviscerated by the controlling obsession of the filmmaker. 'Marker's images thus become "found" images that not only are appropriated, reassembled, and decontextualised but become digitalised, abstracted, and ghostly in their video form' (Russell 1999: 307). Russell does observe that the video-memory of the Zone is not Krasna/Marker's but Hayao Yamaneko's. Yet her insistence on rationalising the film in terms of Marker's intentions leads her to ignore the implications of this difference, to miss the fragility and ambiguity of the Zone as a refuge from time and history. It is true that the film draws to a close with the tensions apparently resolved. The fleeting direct gaze of a woman filmed in the market in Praia can finally be summoned and held beyond its original duration, which was only 'one twenty-fourth of a second, the length of a film frame.' The Zone is presented as a realm in which 'each memory will create its own legend', and everyone will be able to compose their own list of 'things that quicken the heart'. But at the end there is still the possibility of another letter, and the recollection that Krasna once expressed envy of the Zone, perhaps uncertain how far it could really help him to hold the losses of time and the violence of the past at bay.

It is difficult to ignore the working of history as an active, insistent pressure in *Sans Soleil*. The film perceives history as violent rupture and discontinuity, and as the savage movements of reinscription that obliterate one version of the past in favour of another. 'That's how History advances, plugging its memory as one plugs one's ears.' The film concerns itself with a number of specific events in the historical past: the revolutionary struggles of the 1960s, the Battle of Okinawa during the Second World War, the guerrilla war in Cape Verde and Guinea-Bissau that overthrew the colonial rule of Portugal. The voice-over narrates these histories as a succession of sudden breaks, abrupt twists and reversals of fortune. The Ryukyu civilisation of Okinawa is severed, first by Japanese imperial hegemony, then by the US military invasion and postwar Occupation. The initial success of the Cape-Verde/Guinea-Bissau revolution in both driving out the Portuguese, and uniting the two former colonies in a single federation of independent states, disintegrates into bitterness, infighting, factional splits, coups, depositions, exiles, assassinations and tyranny.

What the reflections upon history in *Sans Soleil* ultimately bring into focus is another form of exile: one which is very much a temporal experience, but which is no less concrete and political than enforced geographical displacement. The film invites contemplation of what it is to live through these literal ruptures in the past, to remember both sides of the abyss: how history was before, and what came afterwards to obliterate it. We see footage of a traditional purification ceremony on Okinawa, but are reminded that the world to which it relates is already gone, and that when the priestess who oversees the ceremony dies, there will be no-one to succeed her. The same sequence depicts the Battle of Okinawa as the cause of the rupture, but represents this event through another kind of ceremony, one that erases the Battle itself by acts of commemoration. We see a monument to one of the mass civilian suicides on the island, at the edge of the crevice where two hundred schoolgirls killed themselves with grenades. We learn that visitors have their pictures taken by the monument, and can buy souvenir lighters in the shape of hand grenades from a kiosk. The exilic movement that is traced in *Sans Soleil* in such passages invokes two impossible places at once: the inaccessible past, and the amnesiac present. The film's succession of memory-images are momentary constellations which reveal each of these elements as the necessary condition of the other: there is no memory without forgetting; no forgetting without memory.

To conclude the mapping of *Sans Soleil*'s double journey via nomadism into exile, it is necessary to return to the starting point and reconsider the values of nomadism. The film's expressions of an exilic and melancholy longing to return into the past, are offset by reminders of the positive and necessary human achievements that are gained even in the teeth of history's abrupt and illogical violence – and sometimes as a direct consequence of it. Sandor Krasna records his return to Narita, the object of large-scale organised protests against the building of Tokyo airport in the 1960s and 1970s. We learn that he feels as though he is in *Brigadoon*: everything is the same as it was a decade previously – except for the addition of the airport. But even though the protesters have failed in their objective aim, we are reminded that: 'all they had won in their understanding of the world could have been won only through the struggle.' Krasna is not naïve about the radical movements of the 1960s: he knows that many of them self-destructed in a welter of infighting, that staunch revolutionaries often evolved into capitalism's brightest recruits. But he refuses to be cynical, because he still treasures the energy and commitment of those who 'trembled with indignation every time an injustice is committed in the world'. He writes that 'they wanted to give a political meaning to their generosity, and their generosity has outlasted their politics.' In *Sans Soleil*, the exile of remembering an inaccessible past does not translate straightforwardly into rosy nostalgia for lost Edens. Going back is not merely impossible, it is also undesirable, if viewed from the political and social perspective of struggles for greater freedom and justice, which the film pays tribute to. *Sans Soleil* permits us to grasp that impossible memory will always lure us, but that the terrain we inhabit is time and history, and that in order to live in it, we need constantly to adapt to new horizons, and find ways of making ourselves at home.

Notes

1. This and subsequent quotations from the commentary are from the English language version of *Sans Soleil*, read by Alexandra Stewart.
2. 'Dimanche à Pékin', in Chris Marker, 1961, *Commentaires*, Paris: Éditions du Seuil, p. 39. My translation.
3. See Chris Marker, 'Sans Soleil', *Trafic* 6, Spring 1993, 81. The commentary in the French version of the film is read by Florence Delay. Intriguingly, a Japanese language version of the film also exists, although I do not know what it does to convey a foreign traveller's familiarity with Japan to Japanese viewers.
4. See for example Robert Rosenstone, '*Sans Soleil*: The Documentary as (Visionary) Truth', in *Visions of the Past: The Challenge of Film to Our Idea of History*, Cambridge MA and London: Harvard University Press, 1995, 152–166; Terence Rafferty, 'Marker Changes Trains', *Sight and Sound* (53)4, Autumn 1984, 284–288, reprinted in Kevin McDonald and Mark Cousins (eds), *Imagining Reality: The Faber Book of Documentary*, London: Faber and Faber, 1996, 241–248.
5. As well as its numerous verbal quotations, *Sans Soleil* includes several extracts borrowed from other films. These are listed in the end credits as: Carnival in Bissau (Sana Na N'Hada), Ranks ceremony (Jean-Michel Humeau), Guerilla in Bissau (Mario Marret and Eugenio Bentivoglio), Death of a Giraffe (Danièle Tessier) and Iceland 1970 (Haroun Tazieff). The last of these is mentioned in the commentary as a borrowed extract.
6. There is a significant precedent for this detachment in Chris Marker's 1967 film *Si j'avais quatre dromedaires* [*If I Had Four Camels*]. This work is composed from still photographs taken by Marker during his global travels over the preceding decade, and accompanied by a voice-over in which a fictional photographer and two of his friends – a man and a woman – discuss and reflect on the images. Both friends offer comments and extended internal monologues that are pointedly critical of the photographer's carefree and rather romantic attitude to his subjects.

7. One of the rare private interiors in *Sans Soleil* appears briefly in this sequence: an image of an uninhabited room with a large window that closely echoes the 'real room' shown in *La Jetée*.
8. The appearance of the Zone in *Sans Soleil* heralds Chris Marker's increasing interest in the possibilities of using digital multimedia to approximate the flux of memory, a departure which would manifest itself in the installation works *Zapping Zone* (1990) and *Silent Movie* (1995), the feature film *Level Five* (1996) and the CD-ROM *Immemory* (1997).

References

Bhaba, H. K. (1999) 'Arrivals and Departures', in Naficy, H. (ed.), *Home, Exile, Homeland: Film, Media and the Politics of Place*, London and New York: Routledge/AFI Film Readers, viii–xi.

Bruzzi, S. (2000) *New Documentary: A Critical Introduction*, London: Routledge.

McDonald, K. and M. Cousins (eds) (1996) *Imagining Reality: The Faber Book of Documentary*, London: Faber and Faber, 241–48.

Marker, C. (1961) *Commentaires*, Paris: Editions du Seuil.

Marker, C. (1993) 'Sans Soleil', *Trafic* 6, 81.

Naficy, H. (1993) *The Making of Exile Cultures: Iranian Television in Los Angeles*, Minneapolis and London: University of Minnesota Press.

Peters, J. D. (1999) 'Exile, Nomadism and Diaspora: the Stakes of Mobility in the Western Canon', in H. Naficy (ed.), *Home, Exile, Homeland: Film, Media and the Politics of Place*, London and New York: Routledge/AFI Film Readers, 17–37.

Rafferty, T. (1984) 'Marker Changes Trains', *Sight and Sound* (53)4, 284–88.

Rosenstone, R. (1995) *Visions of the Past: The Challenge of Film to Our Idea of History*, Cambridge MA and London: Harvard University Press.

Russell, C. (1999) *Experimental Ethnography*, Durham NC: Duke University Press.

Welchman, J. (1996) 'Moving images: on travelling film and video', *Screen* (37)4, 336–350.

PART II

TIME

CHAPTER 4

'ISLAND OF TEARS': GEORGES PEREC, ELLIS ISLAND AND THE EXILE'S LOST PAST

Peter Wagstaff

Exile is not a modern phenomenon. It is however one which, since the start of the twentieth century, has been distinguished by its scale. The refugee, the displaced person, the migrant, is the emblematic figure representing what John Berger has called 'the quintessential experience of our time' (Berger 1984: 55). Yet semantic distinctions, revealed in the choice of vocabulary used to describe the phenomenon, underpin an almost limitless range of ordeals and adventures: migration may be forced or chosen, for reasons which are economic or political, from village to city, across frontiers or oceans; the emigrant may recall her or his origins with regret or affection; the immigrant may find welcome or rejection. Exile, though, is perhaps the least ambiguous of words: banished or cast adrift, rootless or homeless, the exile may look back, but must contemplate the impossibility of return. The desire to go back, to rediscover, will have as its focus a place, but also a time, and the despair that comes from the inability to do so is all the greater when both time and place remain not merely inaccessible, but closed to memory. The purpose of this chapter is to explore the way in which one such irrecoverable loss is expressed as a dark shadow cast on perhaps the most familiar story of mass migration.

In 1979 the French writer, screenwriter and filmmaker Georges Perec, in collaboration with director Robert Bober, made a documentary film for French television entitled *Récits d'Ellis Island: histoires d'errance et d'espoir*. The screenplay was subsequently published in book form, in French, copiously illustrated with archive material and stills from the film and, later, in an English-language version as *Ellis Island Revisited: Tales of Vagrancy and Hope*. As Perec's stature has grown in the years following his early death in 1982, so too has the reputation of a film first seen as a relatively minor enterprise – a commissioned film in an ephemeral medium – in the context of Perec's work as a whole. Its declared subject is European migration to the United States in the late nineteenth and early twentieth centuries, and the part played in that process by Ellis Island, the famous transit station at the mouth of the Hudson River. However, Perec invests this familiar story with a range of unanticipated resonances that invite not only a measured re-evaluation of the impact of mass migration on those who undergo it, but also a reinterpretation of the subject in terms of a personal history revisited in allusive fashion in everything he wrote. The result is a sustained reflection, meditation even, on the meaning and consequences of an irretrievable past. Perec subtly transforms a story of migration – the European emigrant becoming the American immigrant – into a narrative of exile, in which a chronicle of optimism, with newly arrived immigrants beginning to construct new lives in a new country, is overlaid with intimations of absence, fear, and loss. Foreshadowing the observation by Stuart Hall that 'migration is a one way trip. There is no "home" to go back to' (Hall 1987: 44), Perec explores the anguish of a lost past, rather than the anticipation of a hoped-for future. The film's title is instructive in this regard. The word 'vagrancy' is more blunt and sociologically weighted than the French 'errance', yet conveys much of the same sense of uncertainty, aimless wandering, lack of direction, nowhere to go. Its counterpart 'hope' has its own ambiguity, particularly in the French form 'espoir', suggesting less an expectant optimism (for which the French 'espérance' would have been more appropriate), than the product of bitter experience and limited expectations against the odds. For the exile, the corollary of hope is despair.

A further comment is called for on the film's French title, which includes the words 'récits' ('tales/narratives') and 'histoires' ('stories'/'histories'). Perec is clearly fascinated by the tales told about and by the early migrants: each has his or her own version of the impact of the Ellis Island experience, as do the second generation Americans who recall their parents' own stories. The ability to narrate the past, and specifically a personal past, based on individual and collective memories, is seen as a vital resource, and the inability to do so is, for Perec, a wound that can never heal. Early in the film's commentary, Perec reflects that every European language had the same phrase to describe Ellis Island, where prospective immigrants were received, assessed, and granted or, in some cases, refused entry: 'Tränen Insel', 'Ile des Larmes', 'Isola delle Lagrime', 'Island of Tears' (Perec 1981, translated by Mathews 1995: 30). The pervasive theme of this film, therefore, lies less in the expectations and prospects of the immigrant than in what the emigrant has left behind, the impact of what the French, in another context, call 'déracinement', uprootedness, loss of a past.

This was a project that Perec, a prolific and adventurous writer bent on expressing himself in as many different forms as possible, was initially reluctant to embark upon. His reluctance was based on his assumption that it offered little more than a pretext for a nostalgic account of an explicitly Jewish experience of migration from Europe to the New World (Bellos 1993: 616). His eventual participation was assured once he recognised the opportunity to explore a number of themes with which he was already preoccupied and which recur insistently throughout his work. Almost without exception these themes have a bearing on the subject of exile, of estrangement, of displacement. They include: the human need for a sense of personal identity based on family, community and a shared tradition; the nature of memory as an enabler of that tradition, and thus as a factor in the creation of identity; the fundamental role of language in the transmission of culture, and thus in the defining of identity, and in providing order and structure for comprehension of a disordered and chaotic world. And finally, the theme of loss, of absence, which may be said to subsume all the other themes: loss of the most personal kind: of family and community, absence of memory, loss of an inherited linguistic tradition. It follows, therefore, that the Ellis Island of Perec and Bober is not an entirely welcoming place.

Perec's world is one of loneliness and abandonment. Paradoxically, much of his work creates an impression that, on the surface at least, is far from pessimistic, as he playfully delights in the intoxicating power of language. For French readers of his work (and for a long time his work seemed scarcely exportable, so bound up was it with the patterns and potential of the French language) he is seen as the impish maker of puzzles, obsessed with word play and with the creation of labyrinthine novels in which formal constraints and a delight in mystification are the main concerns. His membership of the collaborative group of Paris-based writers known as the OuLiPo (Ouvroir de Littérature Potentielle, or Workshop for Potential Literature), which included Raymond Queneau, Italo Calvino and Harry Mathews, the translator of *Ellis Island*), attests to these concerns. However, two brief examples will serve to demonstrate the ways in which this linguistic playfulness, and preoccupation with form, are put to the service of, and frequently mask, themes such as those outlined above. The theme of absence and loss (not to mention mystification and formal constraint) is perhaps most obviously exemplified by Perec's novel *La Disparition* (1969) [*A Void*], the subject of which is the disappearance of a man and then, progressively, of the friends who search for him. An echo of the novel's central content (or absence) can be seen in the formal constraint adopted by Perec: the lipogrammatic omission of the letter 'e' throughout. A further indicative example is his autobiographical novel *W ou le souvenir d'enfance* (1975) [*W or the Memory of Childhood*], which consists of two, parallel but alternating, initially perplexing texts, the first of which concerns a mysterious transatlantic ocean voyage undertaken by, and for the benefit of, a mute child. The voyage is seen as a forlorn and ill-fated attempt to stimulate the child into speech. The shipwreck which ensues brings about the death of all on board, although the child's body is the only one not to be recovered. Uncertainty surrounds his fate.

Two questions arise: why this preoccupation with disappearance, loss, absence? And why the determination to cloak these themes in an aura of playful mystification? The second, parallel text in *W or the Memory of Childhood* provides the clue: in its elliptical, hesitant way it recounts the early years of a child rendered bereft by the loss of his parents. Like so much of his work it represents Perec's attempt to articulate the deaths of his own parents during the Second World War and, specifically, the disappearance and presumed death of his mother at Auschwitz, following internment at the notorious transit camp at Drancy, on the outskirts of Paris, in 1942. Repeatedly, and in a variety of ways, Perec searches for the means somehow to come to terms with that loss while avoiding direct confrontation with a subject so intensely personal. Creativity for Perec appears to reside, at least in part, in the process of encoding personal trauma in narratives with broad, if not universal application.

The themes of identity, memory, language, loss, therefore have a particularly acute resonance for Perec. Born in Paris of first generation immigrant Polish Jewish parents whom he loses in early childhood, his search for an identity founders on a lack of memories, of cultural and linguistic roots, of knowledge of his forbears. His response to this lack is to analyse the nature of memory, to search for evidence of the past, but above all to resist the inclination to recreate and reinterpret the past, or to fill in the gaps, to provide memories where there were none. His script for the film of Ellis Island, which he delivers himself on the soundtrack, illuminates this response in two ways. First, the subject of dereliction and decay was one that appealed to Perec, as it reflected his long-held and deeply-felt preoccupation with the processes of memory, and absence of memory. In evoking the echoing emptiness of the dilapidated Ellis Island buildings in the 1970s he was able to offer a striking correlative to the images of absence and void which underpin much of his work. Second, he came to realise that, in eavesdropping on the stories, told by the American tour guides, of the countless immigrants arriving in America during the early years of the twentieth century, and listening to the first-hand narratives of the immigrant Americans, many of advanced years, whom he interviewed for the film, he was listening to what might have been – but was not – an element of his own autobiography. What if his parents or grandparents had made the trip across the Atlantic to start a new life, rather than succumb to the fate that awaited them in Europe?

While the initial intention of the film appears to have been an attempt to convey the sheer scale of the biggest peacetime mass migration in modern history (the figure of 16 million immigrants passing through between 1892 and 1924 is mentioned), the inescapable underlying theme is the overwhelming impact on individual lives of being uprooted, transported, in fear and uncertainty towards an unknown destiny with sometimes tragic consequences.

The film's opening shots confound expectations: in evoking a place long seen as the epitome of youthful hope in the future, with its teeming arrivals and noisy, confident commitment to the making of America, Perec and Bober offer near-silent scenes of decrepitude and decay. Almost within the shadow of the Statue of Liberty, with all that represents as a beacon of hope, lies the rotting, rusted, half-submerged hulk of the ferry which carried the newly arrived migrants the short distance from Ellis Island to the Battery and New York. It is the emigrant's destination, rather than immigrant's arrival, which captures Perec's imagination. He is not greatly preoccupied with what awaits the migrants once they reach the mainland. Indeed, there is so little mention of the mainland that the island could almost be in the middle of the Atlantic were it not for occasional glimpses of the Statue of Liberty, inaccessibly distant. Ellis Island is seen as an end, not a beginning.

The central stylistic problem confronting Perec is how best to convey the unimaginable scale of the human tide which passed through Ellis Island year after year. His solution is to enumerate, to list, quietly and insistently, the numbers of seaborne migrants arriving from the ports of Europe North and South, West and even East, constructing a painstaking, poignant, repetitive litany of transatlantic departures. Elsewhere Perec writes of the need to define his role as an artist in terms of a kind of realism that avoids the facile obligation to a political commitment or an unrewarding self-reflexivity, both of which had characterised artistic activity in France in the decades following the Second World War.[1] Mastery of a threatening and incomprehensible reality is only to be achieved through the painstaking process of naming, listing, cataloguing. In the illustrated screenplay to *Ellis Island*, first published in French in 1981 and in English translation in 1995, the page layout reflects Perec's creation of a form of expression close to the prose poem:

> five million emigrants arriving from Italy
> four million emigrants arriving from Ireland
> one million emigrants arriving from Sweden
> six million emigrants arriving from Germany
> three million five hundred thousand emigrants arriving from
> Russia and the Ukraine (Perec 1981, translated by Mathews
> 1995: 23)

The litany of arrivals is accompanied by a similarly mesmeric catalogue of the steamship companies and the vessels which plied the Atlantic routes, and of the European ports from which they set sail:

> Year after year, the steamships of
> the Cunard Line, the Red Star Line,
> the Anchor Line, the Italian Line, the Hamburg-
> Amerika Line, and the Holland-America Line
> crisscrossed the Atlantic.

They set out from Rotterdam, from Bremen
and Göteborg, from Palermo, Istanbul, and Naples,
from Antwerp, Liverpool, Lübeck, and Salonika,
from Bristol, Riga, Cork, from Dunkirk, Stettin, and
Hamburg [...]

They were called the Darmstadt, the Fürst Bismarck,
the Staatendam, the Kaiser Wilhelm, the Westernland, the
Pennland, the Bohemia, the Lusitania, the Giuseppe Verdi,
the Thuringia, the Titanic, the Lidia, the Susquehanna ...
(Perec 1981, translated by Mathews 1995: 29)

The recitation of numbers, places, vessels, conveys something of
the scale and heroic grandeur of the enterprise, but it is impossible not to be struck by the apparently gratuitous inclusion in
the above list of the name *Titanic*, not to be reminded of the
sunken hull of the ferry in the opening moments of the film, not
to recall the shipwreck in Perec's autobiographical novel *W or the
Memory of Childhood*. Once again, Perec's Ellis Island is an end,
not a beginning. The ninety-eight per cent of emigrants granted
admission to the United States are of less interest to him than
the two per cent – or two hundred and fifty thousand people –
who were turned away, individual family members shipped
back to their European port of origin. Or the three thousand
who committed suicide on Ellis Island between 1892 and 1924.

As the film progresses, this verbal inventory is replicated in
visual terms by the camera, roaming inquisitively around the
abandoned buildings. Initially, however, the unending recitation of numbers, countries, ports of departure, is in stark contrast to the filmed images of a silent and derelict Ellis Island, as
it stands empty, its echoing halls littered with the detritus of a
long-abandoned site, its grounds and walkways overgrown
with weeds. Here Perec and Bober, in their confrontation of
visual and verbal images, demonstrate an acute sensitivity to
the ways in which lives are reflected in their surroundings, and
buildings absorb and retain the traces of their inhabitants.
Writing of the ability shown by the early French photographer
Eugène Atget, and the Italian film-maker Michelangelo Anto-
nioni, to invest places with the aura of human presence, Ian
Wiblin observes that:

> The buildings seem to simultaneously project a sense of the
> characters' histories and to be knowing of their fate [...] What
> links them [Atget, Antonioni] [...] is the 'presence' of the build-
> ings depicted, whether in the single frame of the photograph or
> in the twenty-four frames a second of the film, often implying

the absent character or story. They share a clarity of vision that
enables the mundane to articulate simultaneously the aspirations and limitations of humanity [...] It is ultimately the architecture itself that has the stored potential to express human
experience and emotion. In images of built space – whether
still or moving – it is the discernible presence of humanity implied by the direct absence of people that is so moving (Wiblin
1997: 109–12).

This contrast, or counterpoint, between actual absence and
discerned presence is at the heart of a film which seeks both to
celebrate arrival and achievement while simultaneously com-
memorating departure and loss.

There are further contrasts, too, in visual terms, between
the colour film of the present, with the camera tracking
unhurriedly across the waterway, the dock, the deserted Immigration Hall, and the intercut black and white archive still
photographs and – very briefly – film, of migrant families
crowding in their hundreds and thousands onto the dockside.
Other photographs from the period, 'fixed forever in their mis-
leading black-and-white obviousness' (Perec 1995: 37) mostly
of individuals or small family groups, notably mother and
child, are not cut into the film but exhibited self-consciously as
part of the scene being filmed, mounted enlargements
propped against a seat or a window, aligned on a wall. The
technique – of a montage of past and present, black and white
and colour, motion picture and still – owes much to the vital-
ity of documentary filmmaking in France during the 1950s,
notably the work of Georges Franju, Alain Resnais and Chris
Marker (Armes 1985: 163–64). In particular, the foregrounding of archive photographs within slow tracking shots which
explore the buildings and dockside is a suggestive pointer to
the interplay between past and present and to the ambiguous
relationship between the still and moving images used to confront the passage of time. Here the historical past is seen
through the immediate, frozen present of the still photograph
(near-iconic images of individual faces photographed by Lewis
Hine in the early 1900s), images ranged against the walls and
on the benches where their subjects had stood and sat three
quarters of a century earlier.[2] In contrast, the present is captured in the transitory medium of film, where every present
instant strains towards an unseen future even while it is drawn
relentlessly into the past. There is no nostalgic backward
glance in this film, but rather a determination to confront the

past in and through the present, while laying bare the impossibility of interpreting traces of past lives.

This preoccupation with the relationship between past and present as reflected in the status of the photographic image is underscored by the publication, in the year in which Perec and Bober's film was broadcast, of *La Chambre claire* [*Camera Lucida*], Roland Barthes's essay on photography which is also an autobiographical meditation on love, loss and death. For Barthes, old – as opposed to contemporary – photographs have the power to elicit in the viewer a response which is based on the unwelcome, and jarring clash of two temporal states. The photographic subject is someone who is now, at the present moment of viewing, dead, but is also, at the present moment of the photograph, going to die: 'there is always a defeat of Time in them: *that* is dead and *that* is going to die' (Barthes 1980, translated by Howard 1982: 96) The evocation of loss, and mortality, which is at the heart of Barthes's text, is strikingly similar to that prompted by Perec and Bober as their camera lingers on the faces of the (long-dead) individuals who stare suspiciously into the lens recording the first moments of their new life. One historical still image in particular from *Ellis Island* encapsulates the painfully paradoxical impact of what Barthes calls the 'anterior future' (Barthes 1980, translated by Howard 1982: 96): a man, woman and child are photographed in silhouette, gazing over the waterway towards the Statue of Liberty, symbol of their future life (the enlarged photograph is filmed against the background of the same waterway, so that the transition beyond the edge of the still image to the undulating water in the moving present is almost imperceptible). The resonance of the image lies in the confrontation of their hopes for the future and our knowledge of their future (but now past) deaths.

If Perec's first recourse in his attempt to convey the enormity of the migrants' experience is to the understated, unemotional recitation of the lists of peoples and places, his accompanying visual strategy is to focus on the simple physical traces of these same people's day-to-day existence on Ellis Island. The camera's slow but persistent exploration of the abandoned buildings and their meagre contents is accompanied by Perec's voice-over commentary which lays bare both the need to show, and the inadequacy of showing. In a series of apparently never-ending tracking shots he simultaneously shows and lists the succession of empty rooms, the endless corridors, the broken but familiar objects which are the last remaining traces of this vast transient population. A white porcelain sink, four chairs, two ironing boards, three sewing machines. Tables, desks, rusted lockers, a large saucepan, a sieve, a wheelbarrow, unfilled forms, a hymnal (see Perec 1981, translated by Mathews 1995: 46).

Even before the renovation that was to turn Ellis Island into a national monument to the immigrant, visitors were given guided tours, treated to the well rehearsed anecdotes. Perec's camera accompanies such a tour group, composed mostly of people whose family history impelled them to seek some insight into a place that marks the starting point for their American existence. But it is also an end point: the end of a previous existence, culture, language. The visiting group is entertained by the doubtless much-repeated tale of the elderly Russian Jew queuing for hours to be processed by the authorities and who, when his turn finally arrives, cannot remember the all-American name (implausibly recorded as Rockefeller) that he has been advised to proffer to speed his acceptance. Instead he mumbles in panic-stricken Yiddish 'schon vergessen' [I forgot already], with the result that he is instantly transformed into the authentically Irish-sounding Sean Ferguson, and the new American existence is gained at the expense of the old identity, culture, language, even name (Perec 1981, translated by Mathews 1995: 19). Even this glibly recounted anecdote serves to reinforce Perec's central preoccupation: the indissoluble link between name, culture and identity, between history and selfhood. He notes in passing that, in 1976 at the time of the American Bicentennial celebrations, 'several dozen Smiths whose families had come from Poland asked to be renamed Kowalski', adding, perhaps unnecessarily, 'both names mean blacksmith' (Perec 1981, translated by Mathews 1995: 20).

At this point in the film a distinction begins to appear between the usual expectations of visitors to Ellis Island and the thoughts of Perec as observer of these visitors. The camera pans across the empty benches, the rusty ironwork, while Perec reflects on the motives which prompt an exploration – one might almost say pilgrimage – to such a place. In his eyes, most of these visitors come for reasons more complex than simply to discover facts about the past:

> they haven't come to learn anything
> but to recover something,
> to participate in something particularly theirs,

some indelible trace of their story
something that is part of their common memory (Perec 1981,
translated by Mathews 1995: 52)

Perec's own motives and reactions are very different:

to me Ellis Island is the ultimate place of exile, that is,
the place where place is absent, the non-place,
the nowhere. [...]
what I find present here
are in no way landmarks or roots or
relics
but their opposite: something shapeless, on the outer edge of
what is sayable,
something that might be called closure, or cleavage,
or severance,
and that in my mind is linked
in a most intimate and confused way
with the very fact of being a Jew (Perec 1981, translated by
Mathews 1995: 58)

For Perec, then, the notion of exile seems to be linked not with
place, or even displacement, but rather placelessness –
absence of place – a condition which would be tolerable if only
there were the memory of an earlier place, or time. Without
memory, there are no roots, no belonging, only exile, and an
irremediable sense of loss.

In *Camera Lucida*, Barthes's reflections point towards a cul-
minating image, constantly alluded to, but never revealed:
that of his mother as a child. Seeking, after his mother's death,
a photograph that will enshrine for him the truth of her existence, 'the impossible science of the unique being' (Barthes
1980, translated by Howard 1982: 71), he nonetheless cannot
evade the traumatic realisation that 'in front of the photograph of my mother as a child, I tell myself: she is going to die'
(Barthes 1980, translated by Howard 1982: 96). The death of
the mother is a theme to which Perec, too, feels impelled to
return, more or less obliquely, throughout his work. One further
photograph among the many historical still images filmed in
Ellis Island seems to echo this concern: the camera scans – in a
painfully slow vertical panning movement – the image of a
small girl who sits patiently, and alone, returning the viewer's
gaze. The child is, probably, about the same age as Perec's
mother would have been. The camera comes to rest, finally, on
the silver dime which the girl clutches between her fingers, the

coin which marks her impending transition to the New World. This is the child that his mother could have been. For Perec, it would seem that these still photographs express both the temporal paradox of unknown lives lived in the retrospective knowledge of their ending, and the deeply personal anguish of an irrecoverable loss.

Perec can perhaps be seen, then, to have encoded, within a widely accessible narrative, elements of a deeply traumatising personal loss. But that is not the full extent of the metaphorical displacement at the heart of *Ellis Island Revisited*. In his detailed delineation of the treatment meted out to emigrants arriving at Ellis Island, the triage processes undertaken to determine those who were deemed fit to be granted access to the New World, Perec sets up a series of unsettling, allusive correspondences with other transit camps, and far bleaker destinations. Whether in the verbal descriptions of the medical examinations to which new arrivals were subjected, with the chalked letter on the lapel to indicate H for heart disease, C for tuberculosis, TC for trachoma, and so on, or in the darkly visual impact of long, slow tracking shots along deserted, barrack-like sheds and endless corridors full of foreboding, this is a film which lies under the shadow of other films of ruined, forsaken places where powerless people were once treated in a less than humane way.[3] Perec has learnt the lesson of filmmakers such as Alain Resnais who, with his seminal film treatment of Nazi atrocities in *Nuit et Brouillard* (1955) [*Night and Fog*], in collaboration with poet and death camp survivor Jean Cayrol, sought simply to show, rather than to explain, interpret or persuade, and whose evocation of the traumatic impact of calamitous events gains a disturbing force as a direct consequence of that visual and verbal reticence.

What, then, is Perec seeking to achieve with his quietly allusive elision of disparate historical events and private trauma? The displacement at work in this film is far from being simply geographical or cultural. It is rather an attempt to discover something that John Berger, another artist much concerned with the plight of the migrant and the exile, has called 'Another Way of Telling'. In exploring Ellis Island and the experiences of those who arrived there, Perec is also exploring the route that led him there, the affinities with his own sense of exile (see Perec 1981, translated by Mathews 1995: 8).

Two poems, one American, one European, both written in the aftermath of catastrophe, explore the impulse to forget, and to remember, in terms which echo the imagery of both

Perec and Resnais. Carl Sandburg's 'Grass' was written in 1917:

> Pile the bodies high at Austerlitz and Waterloo.
> Shovel them under and let me work –
> > > I am the grass; I cover all.
>
>
> And pile them high at Gettysburg
> And pile them high at Ypres and Verdun.
> Shovel them under and let me work.
> Two years, ten years, and passengers ask the conductor:
> > > What place is this?
> > > Where are we now?
>
>
> > > I am the grass.
> > > Let me work
>
> (Sandburg 1970: 1147)

In 1948, to mark the production of his play *Antigone*, Bertolt Brecht offered an alternative perspective in a poem which ends with the lines:

> And you would not let the mighty
> Get away with it, nor would you
> Compromise with the confusers, or ever
> Forget dishonour. And over their atrocities
> There grew no grass
>
> (Brecht 1994: 415)

Perec, like Resnais, was aware that, in reality, the grass continues to grow, forcing its way through the cracked concrete of the Ellis Island dock as it had between the sleepers of the railway track leading into Auschwitz. He was aware, too, that faced with the need to bear witness to the past, the only honest way is to show the dilapidation of the present, and hope for some resonance to occur. Lacking his own history, deprived of family, of the culture and language of his forbears – in short, exiled from his roots – Perec sought repeatedly to explore ways of giving voice to the anguish of that exile, assembling fragments of the puzzle, without laying bare the deeply personal wound at its heart. In appropriating the multiple narratives associated with Ellis Island, he offers fresh and provocative insights into a familiar story, even as he discovers one more metaphor for the expression of a private grief.

Notes

1. See Perec, Georges, 'Pour une littérature réaliste', *Partisans*, no. 4 (April 1962), 121–130, and Bellos, David, *Georges Perec: A Life in Words*, London, Harvill, 1993, 276: '*Realism* was the means by which a writer could gain mastery over the world'.
2. The use of Hine's photographs of migrants on Ellis Island seems particularly appropriate in the context of Perec's and Bober's project: for Hine, who developed a detached and objective style of social photography, 'a picture was a piece of evidence, a record of social injustice, but also of individual human beings surviving with dignity in intolerable conditions' (Meyers, Amy Weinstein, 'Social Photography: Lewis W. Hine (1874–1940)', in Trachtenberg, Alan (ed.), *Classic Essays on Photography*, New Haven, Connecticut: Leete's Island Books, 1980, 109–113 (109).
3. The web of allusive correspondences set up by Perec is far-reaching: the series of questions to which immigrants were subjected – 'Where are you from? How old are you? What kind of work do you do?' (Perec 1995: 16–17) – is eerily reminiscent of the questions recounted by Primo Levi in his testimony of existence at Auschwitz: 'Someone in a brand-new striped suit asks me where I was born, what profession I practised "as a civilian", if I had children, what diseases I had, a whole series of questions' (Levi 2000: 54).

References

Armes, R. (1985) *French Cinema*, London: Secker and Warburg.

Barthes, R. (1980) *La Chambre claire*, Paris: Cahiers du Cinéma, Gallimard, Seuil. English translation by Richard Howard (1982) *Camera Lucida*, London: Jonathan Cape. References cite this edition.

Bellos, D. (1993) *Georges Perec: A Life in Words*, London: Harvill.

Berger, J. (1984) *And our faces, my heart, brief as photos*, London: Writers and Readers Publishing Cooperative.

Brecht, B. (1994) *Poems 1913–1956*, edited by J. Willett and R. Manheim, London: Minerva. Translated from Brecht, B. (1967) 'Antigone', in *Gesammelte Werke*, Band 10: *Gedichte 3*, Frankfurt am Main: Suhrkamp Verlag.

Hall, S. (1987) 'Minimal Selves', in L. Appignanesi (ed.), *Identity. The Real Me. Post-Modernism and the Question of Identity*, ICA Documents 6, London, ICA.

Levi, P. (2000) *If This is a man. The Truce*, London: Everyman.

Meyers, A. W. (1980) 'Social Photography: Lewis W. Hine (1874–1940)', in Trachtenberg, A. (ed.), *Classic Essays on Photography*, New Haven, Connecticut: Leete's Island Books, 109–113.

Perec, G. (1962) 'Pour une littérature réaliste', *Partisans*, no. 4 (April), 121–130.

Perec, G. (1975) *W ou le souvenir d'enfance*, Paris: Denoël. English translation by D. Bellos (1989) *W or the Memory of Childhood*, London: Harvill.

Perec, G. (1969) *La Disparition*, Paris: Gallimard. English translation by G. Adair (1996) *A Void*, London: Harvill.

Perec, G. avec R. Bober (1980) *Récits d'Ellis Island: histoires d'errance et d'espoir*, Television film. Length: 100 minutes. Paris: Institut National de l'Audiovisuel/Editions du Seuil. Part I translated and read by H. Mathews as *Ellis Island Revisited: Tales of Vagrancy and Hope*, Paris: Institut National de l'Audiovisuel and French Foreign Ministry.
Illustrated screenplay originally published (1981) *Récits d'Ellis Island: histoires d'errance et d'espoir*, Paris: Hachette/Le Sorbier. New edition (1994) Paris: P.O.L. English translation by H. Mathews (1995) *Ellis Island*, New York: The New Press. References to the English text are to this edition.

Sandburg, C. (1970) 'Grass', in Margaret Ferguson, Mary Jo Salter, and Jon Stallworthy (eds), *The Norton Anthology of Poetry* (4th Edition), New York and London: Norton.

Wiblin, I. (1997) ' The Space Between: Photography, Architecture and the Presence of Absence', in Penz, F. and M. Thomas (eds), *Cinema and Architecture: Méliès, Mallet-Stevens, Multimedia*, London: British Film Institute, 104–12.

CHAPTER 5

FORCED MIGRATION AND INVOLUNTARY MEMORY: THE WORK OF ARNOLD DAGHANI

Deborah Schultz

The exile experiences a range of interconnected memories – memories from the homeland, perhaps from previous places of exile, as well as short-term memories from the current place of residence. These memories change during time, and become prominent or fade due to experiences in the present. Memories form their own everchanging sequences, and run at their own speeds – sometimes quickly, other times in slow motion or repetitive like a broken spool. The relationship between internal memory and external circumstances, between absence and presence, juxtapose and interact.

Above all, although memories may be called up at will, they often impose themselves upon the mind by force. They appear and reappear, making the past a persistent part of the present. In this way, the forced state of exile is reflected by the involuntary nature of memory. The exile may continue to feel that s/he has no control over either external or internal life.

This paper will examine the relationship between forced migration and the workings of involuntary memory, with regard to representations in the visual arts. Examples will be drawn from the work of Arnold Daghani (1909–85) for whom memories were often strongly manifested as images, flashing in the mind with powerful effect.[1] While Daghani's written

Figure 5.1 'Fragments of Memoirs', 1964, ink on paper, 54 × 33 cm; in *What a Nice World*, 1942–77, 16.

diaries exemplify the desire and need to recall details both from memory and other external sources, his visual works often reveal a lack of control in which images seem to come to mind involuntarily. The relationship between word and image with regard to the event and memory of it, highlighting the nature and limitations of these different forms of representation, underlies the structure of Daghani's work and of this essay.

The notion of 'involuntary memory' is best known from Marcel Proust's experience of eating a madeleine, that returned him directly to his childhood. For Proust, this 'instant' was prompted by the sensation of taste, while for Walter Benjamin, it has been suggested that smell had a comparable effect (Leslie 1999: 116). Benjamin argued that 'true' (in contrast to 'intentional') memory is involuntary and provokes a shock effect. However, what could be described as Daghani's involuntary memories did not seem to come as a shock or instant. Nor were they associated with blissful childhood recollections. Rather, they seemed to haunt his mind; they were involuntary because he could not control them.

For Daghani, then, the past and present of his experiences continued to coexist. His images may be better compared to what Henri Bergson describes in *Matter and Memory* as 'dream-images' that 'usually appear and disappear independently of our will' (Bergson 1911: 97). A number of works by Daghani give visual form to these concerns in which the past is condensed, displaced and firmly imposed on the present.

Historical Context

Arnold Daghani (1909–85) came from a German-speaking Jewish family in Suczawa, in the Bukovina, now Suceava in Romania. Then the Bukovina formed the 'easternmost' part of the Austro-Hungarian Empire, as Paul Celan, one of its best-known names, described the region (Felstiner 1995: 4). The Bukovina was renowned for its cultural life and ethnic diversity, but this character was largely lost due to the effects of the Second World War, and the subsequent split of the region between Romania and the Ukraine, when each part became absorbed by the stronger national identities of these newly defined states.

Daghani's life was structured by a series of relocations that were often due to exterior circumstances over which he had little control. He and his wife Nanino had moved to Czernowitz from Bucharest in the early 1940s when their home was destroyed by an earthquake, and the Soviet occupation of the Bukovina meant that there were incentives to move to the north. However, soon after they arrived, the political situation changed and the Nazis took control in collaboration with the Romanian Fascists. In 1942 Daghani and Nanino were deported from Czernowitz, through Transnistria, and across the river Bug, to the forced labour camp at Mikhailowka in the south west Ukraine. While the camp was run by the SS, the inmates worked for the August Dohrmann engineering company, repairing the main road (the Durchgangsstrasse IV or DG IV) that runs through the region. In April 1943 Daghani and Nanino were commissioned by the engineers to make an eagle mosaic for their regional headquarters in Gaissin. Bizarre as it seems, in the middle of the war, Daghani and Nanino were 'commandeered' to 'embellish' the engineers' garden (Daghani 1961: 57). As there was no transport available to take them there every day from the camp, in June it was decided that they would stay in the garage of the headquarters until the mosaic was completed. There, by chance, they came into contact with a shoemaker and member of the local resistance who suggested that they escape; he arranged for a guide to lead them back across the river Bug, to the relative safety of the ghetto in Bershad where they stayed in hiding for several months until they were taken by the Red Cross back to Bucharest. While in Bershad they heard how, following a partisan attack when some escaped, all the remaining inmates in Mikhailowka were shot. Later they would hear how the shoemaker was also killed.

Back in Bucharest, Daghani lived in ideological exile as his rejection of Socialist Realism, and refusal until 1957 to join the Artists' Union, meant that he was unable to exhibit. Nevertheless, a number of artists and critics visited him and admired his work, including some leading figures on the Bucharest art scene, such as artist and director of the National Museum of Art Max Herman Maxy and the critic Eugen Schileru. Hopes of a better life and greater recognition elsewhere, in the 'Free World' of the Cold War, led Daghani and Nanino to emigrate to Israel in 1958, but only to subsequent disappointment. They had embarked upon a long period of instability in exile. Their hopes and expectations did not materialise, and while Daghani was free to draw in whatever style he wished, his audience was small and his reputation did not develop extensively. From Israel they moved between Jona, a small town in Switzerland, and London, unable to obtain residency permits. Officially stateless, Daghani wrote in despair, 'Which country will receive us? We have too long been standing on one leg. Like me, Nanino is waiting for a miracle to make its appearance round the corner' (Bohm-Duchen 1987: 38).

In 1960 they settled in Vence, in the south of France, where Daghani was supported by the Michael Karolyi Foundation, and they remained there for ten years. At that time Vence was the artistic centre of Europe – Picasso, Matisse, Chagall and other prominent Modernist names lived in the area. However, Daghani felt rejected and excluded from the artistic circles to which he so wished to belong. He had no artistic training and, despite a small but enthusiastic circle of friends and supporters, he always felt like an outsider. A typical experience is summed up in the response of a dealer who told him, 'I like your work immensely, but you can't expect me to run the risk – you've got no name!' (A1004).[2] He was stuck in a vicious circle familiar to so many artists. Meanwhile he received letters from the Romanian art critic Petru Comarnescu, who had always praised his work and told him: 'I thought of suggesting to you to come back to Romania ... You would be among the first and highest artists' (*What a Nice World*: 162). But they did not want to return, and although legally they could stay indefinitely in Vence, Daghani was unable to bear what he described as the '*atmosphère artistique*' (Bohm-Duchen 1987: 40). In 1970 they were granted permission to stay in Jona, but where there was no artistic scene and Daghani was at an even greater distance, both physically and in terms of recognition, from the art world that he had now rejected. In 1977 they were finally granted residence permits in Britain and moved to Hove where they remained until they died – Nanino in 1984 and Daghani in 1985.

Visual Traces of the Past in the Present

Many of Daghani's diaries are based around the period in the Mikhailowka camp from 1942 to 1943 and exist in a number of verbal and visual forms, which he continually remade and rewrote with ever more details, giving a sense of unending circularity that overrides the structural chronology. The proliferation of different formats – published, unpublished manuscripts, handwritten, visual works – adds to this accumulation

Figure 5.2 Untitled [Mikhailowka accommodation], 1943, ink and watercolour on paper with tracing paper, 60 × 42 cm; in *1942 1943 And thereafter (Sporadic records till 1977)*, 1942–77, 115.

of material. Daghani's tireless revisions, in which certain narratives are obsessively recalled and reinscribed again and again, seem to highlight the space between the event, memory, and textual and visual representations. For none of these representations are mimetic, all involve different filters, while even at the time the event is transferred through our subjective responses to which earlier existing memories immediately add further layers of interpretation.

The limitations of verbal communication have been discussed extensively in postmodern theory. While acutely felt by the exile, displaced from the territory of their native language, the survivor experiences even more so the 'necessity' and 'inadequacy' of language (Bartkowski 1995: 129). As both exile and survivor, Daghani seems to have been primarily concerned with telling what happened in any medium, with as many details as possible, obliged to act as a historian to provide 'A Chapter of Contemporary History' that was still largely unknown (*1942 1943 And Thereafter*: A). Daghani's anxieties seemed to have been less with the media and more with the lack of receptive audience.

Daghani made over fifty drawings and watercolours that he smuggled out of Mikhailowka and Bershad, and which can be seen as forming a fragmentary visual diary of the period. Daghani described these works as 'genre' scenes – interiors of the sleeping quarters, inmates at work on the roads, portraits of other inmates. They appear gentle and low key, painted in soft colours and sensitively drawn. Daghani was criticised by some of the other inmates as well as by later viewers of both his written and visual works, for not showing accurately the conditions in the camp. One publisher rejected his written diary on the grounds that there were 'too few atrocities' (Daghani 1961: 5) while to a fellow inmate, poet Selma Meerbaum-Eisinger, 'the [visual] works looked tame, as according to her they did not show sufficient cruelty' (Daghani 1961: 100). Daghani stated that he wished simply to 'depict life in the camp' (Daghani 1961: 100) and had made a conscious decision to portray the dignity of the inmates rather than their beatings and executions which, he felt, 'would certainly lower the almost super-human dignity with which the slaves went to the grave ... why cheapen that by atrocities painted or drawn, even if they surpass imagination and "happen" to be true?' ('Let Me Live' n.d.: 63).

Daghani's work thereby brings into focus the fragmented relationship between the event, its verbal and its visual representations. Whereas his written accounts record many acts of brutality by the guards (although less graphically described than in accounts by many other survivors), Daghani consciously and carefully selected both the subject matter and form of the images he would represent. Crucially, he wrote up the text from notes after he returned to Bucharest, whereas the drawings and watercolours were produced in the camp. As Ziva Amishai-Maisels has indicated, inmates tended to make rather objective recordings due to a necessary repression, for allowing their feelings to be fully expressed while in the camp would have made their traumatic experiences more difficult to survive psychologically (Amishai-Maisels 1995: 50).

Some visual works in particular highlight the processes of time and this fragmented relationship. On a watercolour showing the interior of the accommodation, Daghani notes the water damage that occurred when he and Nanino were wading across the river Bug; the significant point of crossing in their escape between the danger of the Nazi-occupied Ukraine and the relative safety of Romanian Transnistria leaves its mark on the image (*1942 1943 And Thereafter*: 117). Some

Figure 5.3 Untitled [seated on stool], 1972, ink on paper, 60 × 42 cm; in *1942 1943 And thereafter (Sporadic records till 1977)*, 1942–77, 115.

years later, Daghani added a layer of tracing paper, which can be seen as a material metaphor for the layering of memory, on which he noted the names of those depicted. Here Daghani's use of tracing paper was a practical solution. In other works he added semi-transparent paper as a means of combining text and image, a practice that recalls Charlotte Salomon's series of gouaches *Life? or Theatre?* (1942) in which painted inscriptions overlay images in a close integration of the two media.

A 1972 self-portrait of Daghani painting the watercolour adds a further layer to the image (*1942 1943 And Thereafter*: 115). The artist is depicted from behind, as if in his memory he is watching himself working, or even as if he was present as observer of a situation in which he himself had been an observer as an artist. Time becomes fragmented and inter-woven; in this memory he does not recover the scene but adds himself to an enlarged field of vision. The earlier work may have prompted Daghani's memory to produce the later work, helping him to recall the occasion, while the relationship between these works can be seen as indicative of the nature of memory. Even without such prompts, Daghani clearly had a remarkable memory, exemplifying what Lawrence Langer terms the survivors' 'insomniac faculty' in which the process of remembering is not one of reviving decades old memories which may be subject to inaccuracy as 'there is no need to revive what has never died' (Langer 1991: xv).

This latter work also condenses time in the involuntary manner discussed above. For while Daghani is depicted work-ing, the haunting faces of his fellow inmates, killed in the camp, are recalled in light washes, as if present in his memory. Although Daghani states beneath the image that 'The slaves shown are real portraits of them', the faces seem generalised rather than specific (*1942 1943 And Thereafter*: 115). This is also true for a number of other works in which faces are frag-mented and layered, with interconnected frontal and profile portraits. Some faces are barely visible, ghostly, colourless shadows but whose presence seems clearly felt by Daghani. One drawing is structured by the line of the river Bug, beyond which the ghostly faces appear (*What a Nice World*: 394). Beneath this line, Daghani writes:

> Images after the encounter with a World of phantoms
> kept rushing on, superseding and juxtaposing one another.
> Mind trying to sort them out, ordered
> Word to be their spokesman.
> But, alas, Word faded, and
> Images in their oppressive silence
> have since then gone on haunting me.

For Daghani, word seems to represent reason, rationality, con-trol, while images often cannot be restrained. As a result, although many of his visual works were clearly consciously planned, it is in these rather than the written works that the effects of involuntary memory can be most strongly found. On the same drawing, Daghani also identifies with James Joyce's Stephen Dedalus in finding history 'a nightmare from which he was trying to awake' (*What a Nice World*: 394). Word and

Figure 5.4 Untitled [river Bug], 1973, ink on paper, 54 × 36 cm; in *What a Nice World*, 1942–77, 394.

image are also combined in symbolic shapes, representing a language through which Daghani felt his fellow inmates were attempting to communicate with him. As he writes on a 1975 work:

> This is what the victims were dictating me. All hermetic. Their dreams, joys, worries, illusions, hopes, fears, sensual perception, success, failure, tenacity. All were taken into the grave, where they were made to descend. Their lives erased by the wanton pleasure for killing of those aiming at them from the brink of the grave (*1942 1943 And Thereafter*: 10).

There are pages and pages of these hieroglyphic forms, in a number of different works, combining stylised faces and abstract shapes, which are at the same time both words and images. Yet tragically, although Daghani felt that the inmates were dictating to him, their language was hermetic. He sensed their presence but just as their lives were cut short, so communication was fractured and made impossible to decode, resulting in the 'oppressive silence' referred to earlier. While the images discussed above combine memories from the Ukraine with the presence of the inmates, other drawings conflate different temporal periods in Daghani's visual work. The main part of a 1972 drawing, for example, depicts a female, nude apart from sleeves, holding a musical instrument. Daghani made many works on musical themes and drew numerous female nudes throughout his artistic career, but while the two have been brought together in other works, here they are combined with a border of faces looking out from the page that surrounds and encloses the image. Different places and periods are here condensed and conflated in a perhaps unlikely way, suggesting the continuous presence of the faces for Daghani.

For Daghani, then, these faces represent his personal memories, while in the work of other artists, faces or portraits relate to collective memory and function as a means of exploring public responses to contemporary history. It is worth, therefore, considering briefly, examples of works by Christian Boltanski, Anselm Kiefer, Gerhard Richter and Zoran Music in order to indicate the wider context in which to locate Daghani's practice and concerns.

Born in Paris in 1944 on the day the city was liberated, to a Christian mother and a Jewish father, Christian Boltanski describes himself as 'a child of the Holocaust' (Moure 1996: 105). He has also emphasised that 'There's nothing personal

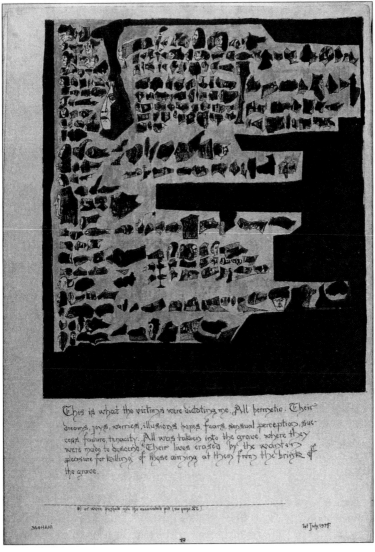

Figure 5.5 Untitled [hermetic language], 1975, ink on paper, 60 × 42 cm; in *1942 1943 And thereafter (Sporadic records till 1977)*, 1942–77, 10.

in my work. Ever' (Garb 1997: 27), for while there are thematic connections with his background, his work is largely about individuals, unknown to the artist and the viewer. Examples from many works made over a number of years, include *Portraits of the Students of the Lentillères College of Secondary Education, Dijon* (1973) and *Altar to the Chases High School* (1988).

Figure 5.6 Untitled [female playing music], 1972, ink and gold paint on paper, 54 × 34 cm; in *What a Nice World*, 1942–77, 10.

Aesthetically, Boltanski's works look incredibly ordered and controlled, examples of Minimalist seriality. However, this contemporaneity is countered by timelessness, by the use of symbols associated with religion, such as small lamps like candles that make the images appear sacred. Boltanski works with black and white portrait photographs, enlarged and closely cropped so that the faces become ghostly, ethereal, distorted like memories. These are not people familiar to the viewer, but are ordinary individuals known to their family and friends and with whom the viewer identifies on this level. Boltanski seems to focus on the face as a means of representing the individual. When an interviewer suggested that Boltanski's work is 'obsessively about the face' he replied that 'The face is so different from person to person. The spirit is revealed in the face. My work is obsessively about people' (Garb 1997: 24).

Boltanski is interested in exploring individuals who do not become known but whose lives are shaped by history – what he describes as '*small memory*. This is what differentiates us one from another. The *great memory* can be found in history books, but the hoard of small bits of knowledge that each one of us has accumulated makes up what we are' (Moure 1996: 108). By contrast, artists such as Anselm Kiefer and Gerhard Richter have depicted the faces of well-known figures as a means of exploring the collective memory of recent German history. In Kiefer's *Ways of Worldly Wisdom: Arminius's Battle* (1978–80) the woodcut portraits of German historical figures were 'according to Kiefer, all based on images reproduced in Nazi mass-market publications' (Biro 1998: 292). The work caused controversy due to this representation of historical figures who had been appropriated to construct a National Socialist identity. Richter's *48 Portraits* (1971–2) can be seen as a highly public form of address as it was commissioned by the West German government to represent the country at the 1972 Venice Biennale. However, the work went beyond an official set of portraits, by reflecting upon individual and collective subjectivity to the extent that it 'suggested that it was no longer possible to construct a coherent cultural canon in West Germany after 1945' (Biro 1998: 177).

Thus these works, by German artists, explore questions of collective memory and postwar national identity. Through art, they examine unresolved issues in cultural representation relating to the wartime period. Another artist who, like Daghani, explored private history and 'small memory', and who also lived for most of his life in exile, without a country's identity to explore, was Zoran Music. Also from the 'Mitteleuropa' of the Austro-Hungarian Empire, from a small town on the Italian-Slovenian border, Music was born in the same year as Daghani (1909) and was interned in Dachau in 1944. Following liberation in 1945 he returned to Venice and previous themes in his work. However, 'the memories of Dachau were intensely present ... And when they first surfaced in his painting they came so indirectly that they took even Music by surprise' (Peppiatt 2000: 11). The effect seems comparable to involuntary memory. As Music has articulated in artistic terms, when asked in an interview about how his images developed, he replied: 'The only worthwhile images are those that come about of their own accord' (Peppiatt 2000: 23) and on another occasion that 'It's always involuntary ... You have to wait for things to come by themselves' (Peppiatt 2000: 34). Thus, in the 1970s, Music began an extensive series of paintings, to which he returned in later phases, titled *We Are Not The Last*, in which piles of corpses are depicted. On many works in the series the paint is applied so lightly and sensitively that, as with Daghani's ink washes of faces, Music's figure is 'insubstantial ... like an apparition ... In a second, it seems, the fragile form will dissolve forever, leaving only the darkness behind' (Peppiatt 2000: 9).

Ghosts and Destiny

Whereas in his written diaries Daghani wished to commemorate his fellow inmates and draw historical attention to the camps in the Ukraine, his images and symbolic language appear to have been more involuntary, arising from his unconscious memory. Both forms of production were also motivated by survivor guilt. As he writes in *1942 1943 And thereafter (Sporadic records till 1977)*, 'Not to this very day have I been able to get rid of the horrifying thought how our fellow inmates were butchered one after another. By right we should have shared their fate' (*1942 1943 And Thereafter*: 214). However, rather than exploring his unconscious, Daghani articulated his activity more as the result of an external power or presence. Beneath a 1971 self-portrait a hand inscribes runic shapes (*What a Nice World*: 67). Above Daghani writes: 'As if a hand had been writing down words whose meaning are lost on – ', the space indicating himself. A second self-portrait is

Figure 5.7 'As if a hand...', 1971, ink and gold paint on paper, 54 × 34 cm; in *What a Nice World*, 1942–77, 67.

drawn on his forehead, as if in his mind. On another drawing a victim is depicted, dictating to Daghani, in a variation on Rembrandt's *The Evangelist Matthew with an Angel Dictating* (*1942 1943 And Thereafter*: 9).

Figure 5.8 With a victim dictating, 1961, ink, felt-tip pen and watercolour on paper, 60 × 42 cm; in *1942 1943 And thereafter (Sporadic records till 1977)*, 1942–77, 9.

Elsewhere this pressure is less clearly defined. As Daghani asks,

> What force, obsession or otherwise has been driving me to allow my mind for twenty-nine years (after our return to Bucharest from Modern Hell) ... to be bent on what took place

there? ... Does it mean that I am seeing myself as a sort of historian in the hope that the documents about what took place
on the DG IV may one day serve as my contribution to the war
years 1942–1943? ('Let Me Live' n.d.: 269)

The overwhelming impression Daghani gives is of his lack
of choice in what he does and, elsewhere, lack of choice in
where he lives; as he writes on a 1961 self-portrait, 'where
shall we be going ... only fate knows' (A1194). So just as external forces (political and predetermining) control where he
lives, so other pressures (both internal and external) determine the nature of his activity wherever he is. On a number of
visual works Daghani expresses his lack of choice at being an
artist, despite the accompanying lack of success. He writes:

> Being an artist is not always enjoyable. Sometimes it is more of
> a duty and has led to my exhaustion at times and possibly my
> ill health... I can't explain why I continue to be an artist. How
> can I? It's just that I am loaded with ideas and must express
> them in visual symbols. I can say no more, predestined to suf-
> fer from the arts (Bohm-Duchen 1987: 71).

While on a 1974 self-portrait he seems to suggest that fate
has determined his misfortune: 'Work, work, work. Working
without the ghost of a chance to meet the right people in the
world of Art; is this my destiny?' (A1213). The impression
given to the viewer is that Daghani neither chose to be an
artist, nor an unsuccessful one. However, it was being an artist
that had indirectly enabled Daghani and Nanino to escape
from and survive Mikhailowka. In his diary Daghani remembers the Romanian policeman who issued their deportation
order in Czernowitz and who advised him to take his watercolours to Mikhailowka. Daghani records that he told the
policeman, '"We are being sent to death and you expect me to
take them? To what use?"' But the policeman was insistent:
'"To what use?" he answered back. "They might just save both
your lives; one never can tell." As I went on being refractory,
he made Nanino open the rucksack, and both sketchbook and
colours were placed on top' (Daghani 1961: 62–4). Daghani
became known in the camp as an artist and the guards commissioned him to work on artistic projects such as the eagle
mosaic, that led to his and Nanino's escape. But Daghani did
not wish to take the watercolours, nor did he intend to try and
escape until a plan was offered to him. In each case he regards
himself as the passive responder to another's initiative. While

the location in which he lived was largely outside his control, so too was his activity and his success as an artist.

At the same time, Daghani's extensive production of self-portraits and diaries seems to suggest a highly constructed self-image. Both images and written works, including auto-biographical albums of photographs (personal and of artworks) and other documentation (letters, reviews and photocopies of these), are extensively annotated with Daghani's comments, often added on different occasions. The effort put into these works seems to suggest that Daghani was very conscious of his public image, both during his lifetime and how he would appear in posterity. That his diaries were written largely in English, also seems to indicate an awareness of the audience to which he wished to communicate, as well as perhaps a distancing from his origins.

Although being an artist meant that Daghani survived the camp and did not suffer the same fate as his fellow inmates, he would spend the rest of his life suffering for his art, fulfilling the role of the neglected avant-garde artist. To some extent, Daghani seems to fit into Donald Kuspit's definition of the 'personalist artist' who 'argues that art is a special way of suffering, one that assures us – demonstrates – that if one suffers properly one can have a higher self. The personalist artist offers himself as the exemplary sufferer' (Kuspit 1993: 292–3). However, Daghani's artistic angst was coupled with haunting memories from other times and places that add external dimensions to his suffering. His experiences, then, were twofold: he was an outsider not only as an artist but also as an exile, and he suffered as an artist as well as for his memories. He was forced to be an exile for most of his life, due to external circumstances and internal pressures, while much of his activity would commemorate his fellow inmates, both consciously and involuntarily, with written works to ensure that they would not be forgotten by history, and visual images imbued with their memory and a sense of their continuing presence. But while Daghani continued to add to his diaries and remake images from the past, the aim of completion was always unattainable.

Notes

1. An extensive collection of over 6,000 works by Arnold Daghani, including drawings, writings, folios and documentation, forms the Arnold Daghani Collection at the University of Sussex, and includes the following unpublished works and manuscripts referred to in this chapter: *What a Nice World* (1942–77); *1942 1943 And thereafter (Sporadic records till 1977)* (1942–77); 'Let Me Live' (n.d.). The only published work cited by Daghani is *The Grave is in the Cherry Orchard*, London, Adam: 1961, referred to in the text as (Daghani, 1961).
2. Catalogue numbers refer to individual works as catalogued in the Arnold Daghani Collection.

References

Amishai-Maisels, Ziva (1995) 'Art Confronts the Holocaust', in Bohm-Duchen, M. (ed.), *After Auschwitz: Responses to the Holocaust in Contemporary Art*, Sunderland and London: Northern Centre for Contemporary Art, in association with Lund Humphries, 49–77.

Bartkowski, Frances (1995) *Travellers, Immigrants, Inmates: Essays in Estrangement*, Minneapolis, MN: University of Minnesota Press.

Bergson, H. (1911) *Matter and Memory* [1896], translated by Nancy Margaret Paul and W. Scott Palmer, London: Allen and Unwin.

Biro, M. (1998) *Anselm Kiefer and the Philosophy of Martin Heidegger*, Cambridge and New York: Cambridge University Press.

Bohm-Duchen, M. (1987) *Arnold Daghani*, London: Diptych.

Daghani, Arnold (1961) *The Grave is in the Cherry Orchard*, London: Adam.

Felstiner, J. (1995) *Paul Celan: Poet, Survivor, Jew,* New Haven and London: Yale University Press.

Garb, Tamar (1997) 'Interview. Tamar Garb in conversation with Christian Boltanski', in Semin, D., T. Garb and D. Kuspit (eds), *Christian Boltanski*, London: Phaidon, 6–43.

Kuspit, D. (1993) *Signs of Psyche in Modern and Postmodern Art*, Cambridge and New York: Cambridge University Press.

Langer, L. L. (1991) *Holocaust Testimonies: The Ruins of Memory*, New Haven and London: Yale University Press.

Leslie, E. (1999) 'Souvenirs and Forgetting: Walter Benjamin's Memory-work', in Kwint, M., C. Breward and J. Aynsley (eds), *Material Memories*, Oxford and New York: Berg, 107–122.

Moure, G. (1996) *Christian Boltanski: Advent and Other Times*, Barcelona: Editions Polígrafa and Santiago de Compostela, Centro Galego de Arte Contemporánea.

Peppiatt, M. (2000) *Zoran Music*, unpublished Exhibition Catalogue, Norwich, Sainsbury Centre for Visual Arts, University of East Anglia and London: Estorick Collection of Modern Italian Art.

CHAPTER 6

CHANTAL AKERMAN:
A STRUGGLE WITH EXILE

Lieve Spaas

The rapid advances in visual technology offer seemingly end-less possibilities for image creation so that, increasingly, human perception is subjected to a proliferation of external stimuli. How does the viewer react to the visual engulfment that this proliferation of images brings about? Confronted with teeming constellations of images, the viewer is faced with two fundamental aspirations: the first stems from the need to discern formal coherence, the second from the need to locate oneself through memory. Images unfolding on the screen inevitably call for some kind of narrative logic even if, increasingly, visual media construct and deconstruct images in a playful way and, therefore, move away from any kind of formal coherence. Similarly, the effects of new technologies on human memory are considerable and often lead to the viewer having to construct an internal space of exile.

Kaja Silverman argues that whereas 'the moving image consigns what it depicts to oblivion, the still photograph gives us access to a stable and durable image of self' (Silverman 1996: 198). If this were so, the moving image would find itself in a permanent dilemma: either it leaves the viewer with a sense of exile or it configures exile through its own medium and, in this way, offers the viewer a response to the fractured experiences frequently associated with digital art and visual media. Concern with this visual exile underlies the work of

Belgian filmmaker Chantal Akerman. I shall select represen-
tative films from her œuvre and show how they attempt to
engage the viewer in a twofold struggle against exile, operating on both the aesthetic and formal level of film and on a historical level foregrounding the effect of memory.

Akerman began making films when she was only eighteen.
Although she had initially planned to become a writer, seeing
Jean-Luc Godard's *Pierrot le Fou* made her change her mind.
Her first film, *Saute ma ville* [*Blow Up my Town*] (1968), already
addresses the dichotomy between the photographic and the
cinematic image. A gag-like sequence at the beginning of
the film offers a humorous reflection on the moving image. A
young girl enters a high-rise building; impatient when the lift
fails to function, she runs up the stairs humming a song; the
higher she climbs, the slower she hums. A crane shot captures
her ascent as if she herself were a lift. This accelerated image
contrasts with the photograph pinned on the door inside
the flat underneath which is written 'c'est moi' ['that's me'].
Does the still photograph, as Silverman argues, 'give a more
durable image of self'? This may be questioned in Akerman's
film since, by setting fire to the photograph, the girl in the flat
destroys this image of durability.

Is it that Akerman accepts, when she decides to become a
filmmaker, that self-representation will have to find expression in the moving image rather than in photography or writing? In this short, thirteen-minute film, she touches on the
question of representation of the self. The self seems to be striving for recognition (staring in the mirror, writing 'c'est moi'),
but then the girl stages and carries out her own death by blow-
ing up the flat. This early experimental film may question the
'death' of the still image but, since representation of one's own
death is the ultimate act of self-expression, the young Akerman
succeeds in heralding the visual technology as a means of
doing precisely that.

It is already clear, in this first film, that Akerman is engaged
in reflecting on the moving image. This concern also underlies
many of her subsequent films, in particular, *News from Home*,
Hôtel Monterey, *Jeanne Dielman, 23 Quai du Commerce, 1080
Bruxelles* and *Les Rendez-vous d'Anna*. In all of these she addresses
the exile that technological advances have imposed. Her single
point of view, presented through fixed camera or slow lateral
panning, long takes with little or no action and the introduction of a real experience of duration, constitute a rethink-
ing of filmic language and a struggle against the spectator's

undiscerning absorbing of the images that scurry onto the screen.

These films display an endeavour to restore the pre-cinematographic image and address the viewer's unwitting sense of exile when ensnared by a plethora of tantalising images. The new technologies may leave the viewer exiled from the image, from what we imagine a 'pure' image to be, hence Akerman's attempt to keep the viewer's gaze engaged in the act of seeing by the frequent use of a fixed camera that lingers on the image.

In the sixty-three minute silent film *Hôtel Monterey* (1972), for example, an immobile and frontally placed camera emphasises lines, frames and emptiness by filming the hotel entrance, its corridors, the interior of a room, and the lift, by staring, as it were, at its slow ascent and descent, offering an exploration of depth, height, width, verticality, immobility and slow motion. The viewer, like the people in the hotel, waits for its return and for a glimpse of the passengers through the round glass pane in the door, reminiscent of the eye of the camera.

Jeanne Dielman (1975), a memorable two hundred minute film that shocked the film world at the time, also arrests the viewer's gaze in the act of seeing. It captures the daily tasks of a Brussels housewife over a three-day period. Frontal camera angles, the absence of reverse shots and the lengthy showing of the daily actions and gestures of this Brussels housewife give the impression of a presentation of life rather than a representation. For example, when Jeanne prepares the coffee for breakfast, the camera not only renders the various movements and gestures within the duration of real time, it also makes the viewer wait with the eponymous housewife for the filter coffee to drip into the pot. It is clear that the representational value of cinema is questioned here. Does this cinema of duration provoke a sense of alienation or does it make the viewer aware of the delusion present in traditional narrative film? There is a concern here with the aesthetic of the image as well as with filmic narrative.

The well-known opening of Akerman's *Les Rendez-vous d'Anna* powerfully demonstrates the effect of this cinema of duration where the shot, taken with a fixed camera, placed centrally on the platform of a station, lasts and lasts. As Akerman says herself, 'it is not possible to escape from the image when you are placed in front of a fixed image or one where the camera pans slowly laterally' (Aubenas 1995: 6).

What we see here is a deliberate attempt to keep the spectator's gaze firmly anchored in the camera's point of view and to avoid establishing shots from that of different characters. It is as if this kind of filming wants to undo the work of the camera, to make the viewers very conscious of the loss of a real image. Akerman's cinema, then, aims at repairing the viewers' exilic experience from their own vision.

In effect, though, Akerman's films make the viewers intensely aware of their own spectatorial presence. If 'normal' films alienate the viewers from the act of seeing, Akerman's elicit a strangeness and create a different kind of alienation, one that emerges from the split between the eye's ability to perceive – and retain – an image and its transmission to the brain. Her films introduce a slow motion in that transmission that provokes a kind of stasis in the viewer who, accustomed to fast-moving images in a highly visual culture, cannot but feel disoriented in this cinema of duration.

It is clear that in these films Akerman wants to break away from the exile that technological advances have imposed: the multitude of images projected on the screen from a variety of often unidentifiable points of view inevitably produce a visual distortion. Akerman's single point of view, consistently presented through fixed camera or slow lateral panning, constitutes a correcting of this distortion.

Akerman's attempt to break away from the hegemony of the visual technology can be considered as her first confrontation with exile because the struggle in her films is twofold. The first operates on the aesthetic and formal level of film and resides in her style of filming; it aims at creating an image that is not endowed with multiple points of view and does not attempt to force meaning. Instead, it simply pays 'social attention', acts as a presence without seeking to interpret. The second struggle foregrounds a historical exile, that of a world history, which includes her own. For Akerman, a film is, in the first instance, autobiographical; not in the sense of telling events that happened, but inspired by the self, rooted in memory, and by a past that it does not actually narrate.

Indeed, equally central to Akerman's images is the importance of memory as part of a process of recognition and of making meaning when looking at images. The fractured experiences the new technologies frequently introduce affect the work of memory and so hinder the viewers' sense of identity leaving them with a further exilic experience. Memories are powerfully embodied in Akerman's films and require the viewer to engage with the process of memory: memory as personal and cultural history, memory as inscribed in objects and memory as part of a process of making meaning in the work. This is not surprising given that it is through memory that we locate ourselves.

Akerman talks openly about her family background, which constitutes the backdrop of the East–West and West–East trajectories that haunt several of her films. Her parents were displaced Polish Jews who settled in Belgium. In several interviews she has pointed out that her mother was in Auschwitz, but would never speak about it. It seems that these repressed memories emerge in the second generation. Akerman sees her parents as well integrated in Belgium; according to her they do not have a feeling of exile but it seems that she represents the generation in which what was repressed re-emerges. Three films that are rooted in memory, and in which feelings of exile surface or resurface, are *News from Home* (1976), *Histoires d'Amérique* (1989) and *D'Est* [*From the East*] (1993). An East–West trajectory underlies the first two films; a West–East trajectory the last one.

In *News from Home* (1976), set in New York, images of the city of New York are shown, while Akerman reads the letters that her mother wrote from Brussels when, in 1972, she left her home town rather unexpectedly. The letters express the mother's pain at her daughter's unannounced departure and, therefore, encapsulate a feeling of separation from both the East, from where she came, and the West to which her daughter travelled. Random noises interfere with the ability to hear the letter while anonymous images of New York appear on the screen. As Margulies writes, 'The alienation between image and sound parallels the disjunction between the mother's space of writing and Akerman's space of performance – between the foreign reality and New York' (Margulies: 1996, 152).

The axis from East to West is repeated in *Histoires d'Amérique* (1989) where Akerman follows the lives of Eastern European Jews trying to make a new life for themselves in New York. The film is a compilation of stories told by people, uprooted from their native country and language. It reflects the massive waves of Jewish migrants who, at the turn of the century fled from the persecution and oppression they suffered in Russia and Poland and settled in the United States. These migrants found common ground for their conversations. Food, family and philosophy formed the basis of a shared community, a community that did not have to remember the Holocaust in

Europe. However, for the present-day viewer, these images inevitably and, perhaps, more powerfully, also evoke the twentieth-century diaspora.

The trajectory from East to West will be reversed in Akerman's film, *D'Est* [*From the East*], in which she undertakes a journey from West to East. *D'Est* is neither a documentary (there is no commentary) nor fiction (there is no story). Crowds of people either ignore the presence of the camera or react only vaguely to it. There is no narrative structure, Akerman has filmed what attracted her eye or what happened to be there in front of her. In this film, Akerman's two modes of struggle with exile come together. The aesthetic is present in her style of filming and the historical lies in the journey itself, that is to say, in the attempt to reverse history, as it were, and to annul the experience of exile.

D'Est starts with the end of the summer in East Germany, then moves further east, across fields and roads, ending in winter in a cold and snow-covered Moscow. People seem perpetually on the move, carrying packages and marching in the snow toward an unknown destination. This is also the place from where her grandparents and parents came and to which Akerman returns, a reversal of the route travelled by them long ago. In this journey, she does more than attempt to reverse the exile of her family, she also instils a feeling of exile in the viewer. A deep sense of history emanates from images where geographical boundaries are not clear. Long shots of people walking, accompanied by ongoing sounds but without words, unfold on the screen. It is difficult to know where exactly we are, what the crowds are waiting for, where the people are going. Displacement seems at the heart of this film, in which people move or wait in order to go somewhere, but that 'somewhere' is neither defined nor elucidated. The viewer, who comes to feel like a foreigner, out of place, experiences resonances of a tragic history and mass exile.

This is Eastern Europe as Western viewers have come to perceive it, a region where crowds and crowds move and move about, communicating little or not at all, engaged simply in the activity of survival, where people all look similar, all blending in an anonymity that conforms to the Western stereotype of Eastern Europe, all wearing similar fur hats and overcoats. But Akerman dispels the uniformity, which the West has come to associate with Eastern Europe, by breaking away from the crowds and by singling out individuals engaged in their daily routine, in mundane tasks or pleasures, or, who look into the camera, directly engaging the gaze of the spectator. In her notes, taken during the shooting of the film, Akerman wrote: 'I will show faces that ... express something still untouched and often the opposite of that uniformity that at times strikes you in the movement of crowds and erase for an instant the feeling of loss, of a world at the edge of an abyss, a feeling that grabs you when you cross from the East, as I just did' (Margulies 1996: 201). Yet the gaze from within the image itself creates a face-to-face confrontation that arouses the discomfort and unease of the spectator and imbues the viewer's gaze with a sense of voyeuristic embarrassment.

In addition to the strategies used to grapple with exile, Akerman also re-creates the physical experience for the viewers through the use of a multimedia installation. In fact, the film *D'Est* is only part of a multimedia installation for which the full title is *Bordering on Fiction. Chantal Akerman's D'Est*. More than a film, it is an event. It makes use of three different rooms: in the first, the film is shown uninterruptedly against one of the walls. Three rows of eight seats limit the number of viewers to twenty-four, a number which is equivalent to the twenty-four images projected per second on the screen. In the second room, that number is repeated: this time there are twenty-four television monitors, placed upon stands, again in three rows of eight. Instead of sitting down to watch the screen, the spectators must walk between the rows of monitors and catch glimpses of the images as they appear on each of the screens. These images, edited into sequences of four minutes, are identical to the film projected in the first room, but here they are fragmented in such a way as to create visual echoes from one monitor to the next.

The spectators move slowly between the monitors in this second room, watching the incessant walking of the people on the screen. Notions of exile, home and diaspora are evoked by this walking which the viewers have to undertake and which is redolent of the recurrent displacement of the Jewish people. The very fragmentation of the images, by means of the twenty-four monitors, elicits a sense of a tragic past scattered across the desolate torn map of Europe.

Then, in the third room, entitled 'the 25th screen', a final screen, placed on the floor, shows a 25th image, the one in excess of the normal twenty-four images per second, the non-existent, impossible and redundant image. Here a 25th image is shown, but with the image so magnified that it is blurred and nothing specific can be recognised. Here the spectators take their places on cushions on the floor in front of the blurred picture. From two small loud speakers, also placed on the floor, Akerman's voice is heard, reading from Exodus, Chapter 20, Verse 4 in Hebrew and French: 'Thou shalt not make unto thee any graven image, or any likeness of anything that is in heaven above, or that is in the earth beneath, or that is in the water under the earth.'

This calling into question of the creation of images and evoking the biblical prohibition against making images closes the media installation and leaves the viewer with a profound experience of exile, both aesthetic and historical. It is through her wilful transgression of the Biblical command that Akerman stages her twofold struggle with and against exile.

References

Aubenas, J. (1995) *Catalogue des films de Chantal Akerman* (R. Dehaye, ed.), Bruxelles: Commissariat Général aux Relations Internationales de la Communauté Française de Belgique.

Margulies, I. (1996) *Nothing Happens: Chantal Akerman's Hyperrealist Everyday*, Durham and London: Duke University Press.

Silverman, K. (1996) *The Threshold of the Visible World*, New York and London: Routledge.

CHAPTER 7

MEMORY AND EXILE IN THE BILL DOUGLAS *TRILOGY*

Christine Sprengler

Articulating the nature of the relationship between history and memory has for a long time preoccupied academic debate and, given the recent developments in communications, representation, and data storage technologies, will continue to do so in the years to come.[1] Of particular interest to those engaged in such debates are the changes in the perception of history and the expansions to our conception of memory. While historiographical projects subject history to scrutiny, exposing its methodological habits and predilections and proposing new avenues of historical investigation as well as ways of recording the past, research into memory is vast and diverse and includes, for example, trajectories concerning personal memory, collective memory, popular memory, cultural memory, prosthetic memory, and the distinction between involuntary memory and recollection (see, for example, White 1973, LaCapra 1985, Huyssen 1995, Yates 1996). The work of film theorists has certainly contributed much to the developments in these areas. Cinema's recreations of the past have yielded discussions regarding the manipulation of history, the limits of film's ability to document history, and the social and cultural consequences of the reproduction and rehearsal of collective memories (see, for example, Buck-Morss 1994, Radstone 1995, Monk and Sargeant 2002). In contemplating the relationship between memory and history with respect to the cinema, Thomas Elsaesser sketches out one possible role for memory. He observes that,

> As history evaporates, becoming in the process the very signi-
> fier of the inauthentic, the false and the falsifiable, memory
> has gained in status, as the repository of genuine experience,
> the last refuge of what inalienably makes us who we are. [...]
> By marking what is personal about the past, by bearing witness
> and giving testimony, such films add a new dimension to mem-
> ory, connecting the speaking subject to both temporality and
> morality, creating 'pockets of meaning', in the sense one can
> speak, in a guerrilla war, of 'pockets of resistance'.
>   Remembering, giving testimony and bearing witness can be
> tokens of a fight not only against forgetfulness, but also against
> history (Elsaesser 1999: paragraphs 5–7).

The use of memory as a weapon against history is evident in the work of Scottish filmmaker Bill Douglas.[2] Whereas mainstream films often ask the spectator to share in the expe-rience of *collective* memories, memories sanctioned by official historical discourse, Douglas asks the spectator to respond to depictions of his own *personal* memories and, in doing so, chal-lenges the audience to contemplate the very nature of memory itself. The focus of this paper is Douglas's autobiographical *Trilogy* and the ways in which he constructs, both narratively and aesthetically, his personal memories of exile and exclu-sion. The *Trilogy* is a complex work that resists easy categori-sation and interpretation. It is at once a search for home and the experience of belonging and a condemnation of the tyranny that can mar collective units including the home, the community, and the nation. It explores how exclusion from spaces and events generates not only a desire for inclusion, but additional experiences of exile as well. For Douglas, banish-ment from certain spaces and events precludes sharing in the memories associated with these spaces and events and thus precludes participation in history. I will begin this case study with a synopsis of the *Trilogy* and an examination of the importance of memory to Douglas, followed by an analysis of how deliberate juxtapositions of personal and collective memories serve to illustrate his own experience of exile. I will conclude by considering how the Bill Douglas *Trilogy* might be interpreted as a cinematic attempt to re-inscribe into history personal memories as generated by the experi-ence of exile, and thereby to expand and enrich our conception of history.

Printed in high contrast black and white, and with a total running time of nearly three hours, the *Trilogy* documents Douglas's life between 1945 and the mid-1950s. The first part, entitled *My Childhood*, was released in 1972, followed by *My Ain Folk* in 1973 and *My Way Home* in 1978. A conventional synopsis might include the following events: Jamie (as Bill Douglas) is an unhappy illegitimate child of seven or eight living in poverty in Newcraighall (a Scottish mining village) with his cousin Tommy and their maternal grandmother. His mother is institutionalised and, initially, his paternity is unknown. He finds a temporary father figure in Helmuth, a German prisoner of war (POW), but the announcement of Allied victory signals an abrupt end to their relationship. Helmuth's departure leaves Jamie deeply traumatised and before he has a chance to heal, he suffers a further loss with the death of his grandmother. The absence of a legal guardian means the inevitable arrival of state officials and, as Tommy is forcibly removed from the flat, Jamie manages to escape to the house that Tommy had just revealed as the residence of Jamie's biological father and paternal grandmother. Reluctantly they permit him to stay, but they clearly resent his presence up until the moment he too is sent to a children's home. His stay in this institution is relatively uneventful, marked by an unsuccessful foster care placement and a part-time job. At one point, his father's sense of guilt inspires him to bring Jamie back to Granny Douglas's house, a move which proves temporary and which exposes him to further tragedy and abuse. By the mid-1950s he reaches the age for National Service and, as a result of the Suez crisis, is stationed in Egypt. Here Jamie befriends Robert and, as his time in the Service comes to an end, so too does the *Trilogy*. However, although this brief synopsis may convey the main events in the narrative, to describe the *Trilogy* as constituted or structured by these events is to misrepresent Douglas's project since what is of actual importance to him, of course, is how he translates these events to the screen and how, in so doing, he requires us to reinterpret the meaning of historical benchmarks such as the Second World War and the Suez Crisis, to discount their official significance, and instead to experience the particular potency of that which is distinctive and personal.

Douglas employs a number of aesthetic and narrative strategies to privilege the fragmentary and sometimes elusive nature of personal memory over the simplified and often sanitised nature of collective memory. The amount of screen time devoted to the representation of his personal memory displaces recognisable historical events to the margins. The cinematography confirms this, offering additional clues that reveal precisely how Douglas values the personal over the collective. For example, images of villagers rejoicing at the Allied victory are filmed in an extreme long shot, the individual figures barely discernible against the night sky, while in the foreground rages a bonfire that prevents the camera/viewer from getting close enough to participate in the celebration. Quite uncharacteristically, the camera begins to move, zooming in, tilting up, then down, and panning left, ostensibly in an attempt to get around the flames. However, the fire remains centred in the frame, personalising the experience and separating the spectators physically so that, like Jamie, they too are held emotionally at a distance from the action. The result is a cinematic moment that feels empty and remote.

In striking contrast to this, scenes that document very personal memories are saturated with emotional energy. They have a poetic quality that engages the viewer, and they materialise and then fade from the screen in a way that mimics the nature of memory. John Caughie describes the *Trilogy* as composed of scenes that have a 'surreal quality', that exist like fragments of memory, often isolated from one another (Dick, Noble and Petrie 1993: 201). Some images linger, while others disappear prematurely, and rarely is any explanation given for why radical shifts in mood occur. Tommy's vicious attack on Jamie cuts to the boys sitting peacefully with their Granny in the living room. Firelight reflecting off their pallid faces provides the only hint of movement for the first thirty-six seconds of the scene. Then, in a medium shot from behind, Tommy's arm comes to rest across Jamie's shoulders. This incredibly gentle gesture lasts just four seconds and its unexpectedly sudden end leaves the viewer feeling cheated, just as Jamie himself is so often cheated out of the compassion he deserves but all too infrequently receives. The brevity of this moment affords little reprieve from the emotional fluctuations that Jamie and, by extension, the viewers are forced to endure. However, editing alone is not responsible for the fragmentary quality of this scene. A stationary camera and minimal movement within the frame evokes the still photograph, and (the use of lengthy shots notwithstanding) the absence of cause and effect in the sequence creates a montage effect.[3] Mick Audsley, the editor for *My Way Home*, explained that this effect results from Douglas's tendency to 'tell stories with emotional rhythms and not the action rhythms of cinema' (quoted in Dick, Noble and Petrie 1993: 169). By resisting such 'action rhythms', Douglas preserves both the fragmentary quality and the poetic and emotional potency of personal memory, thus avoiding the simplification and clarification required for the particular to become emblematic.

To maintain the uniqueness of each memory, Douglas strove for mnemonic fidelity. That is, he sought to re-create precisely the look and feel of his childhood. In order to accomplish this, he filmed exactly where the events had originally taken place, using for props the actual objects that he had saved, and refusing to give actors a script for fear they might attempt to reinterpret his work through performances. Douglas was notoriously difficult to work for even, on one occasion, firing his assistant director for failing to acquire the right type of jam jar (Dick, Noble and Petrie 1993: 136). Brand Thumin, his editor on *My Childhood*, and assembly editor on *My Ain Folk*, explained how Douglas's obsession with reconstructing his past as faithfully as possible led him to create material that he was subsequently unable to look at. The images he had created, Noble explains, left him 'deeply shaken', and impelled him to discard some very powerful footage (Dick, Noble and Petrie 1993: 144). Peter West, his editor on *My Ain Folk*, offers a similar observation, claiming that '[Douglas] became more and more obsessive about certain aspects of the film that were to do with his own inability to dissociate himself from the actual life that he lived and the artefact he created. This caused him to ask for scenes to be cut or dropped. For example, the father he had created on screen so disturbed him that he wanted the role diminished' (quoted in Dick, Noble and Petrie 1993: 146).

Given Douglas's obsession with mnemonic fidelity, it is significant that one of the prominent characters in the film – Helmuth, the German prisoner of war – is an invention and not an actual figure from Douglas's past. Helmuth's contributions to the narrative give crucial insight into Douglas's conceptions of memory and exile, and his function within the *Trilogy* is threefold: he represents the home that Jamie constantly searches for; he helps to articulate what, for Jamie, is the incompatibility of the personal and the collective; and, as an actual exile, he alerts us to Douglas's concern with the theme of exclusion. First, it is important to recognise that Helmuth's 'meanings' derive in part from his fictionality or invented status. There are, for example, hints very early on in the *Trilogy* that he is merely a construct of Jamie's imagination. For the most part, the audience never knows more than Jamie; he is the narrative focaliser in both perceptual and psychological terms, as we are expected to identify with his perspective and to experience the world as he does.[4] At one point, Jamie watches from a distance as miners and their children are reunited after the day's work. We see expressions of delight as the youngsters are hoisted onto their fathers' shoulders. Yet although this is shot from Jamie's point of view, as viewers, we are aware that, from Jamie's position, it would actually be impossible to see their faces. This jovial familial bonding that Jamie witnesses is immediately replayed in the following scene, but this time between Helmuth and Jamie himself. Here, upon finishing work in the field, Helmuth walks over to Jamie, lifts him over the fence and then crouches down to allow the child to climb onto his shoulders. The two scenes clearly reveal that Helmuth represents the father that Jamie longs for. With the emptiness left by Helmuth's departure, the search for home and a sense of belonging that he had represented becomes the central theme of the film.[5]

Second, Helmuth serves to introduce a recurring theme in the *Trilogy*: the juxtaposition of collective and personal memories in a way that privileges the personal and stresses the incompatibility of such memories (as perceived by Jamie/Douglas) with the collective. This is most forcefully suggested through Jamie's inability to share in the emotional turns of the Second World War. Helmuth is a German POW and thus officially, in 1945, Jamie's enemy. However, not only is Helmuth Jamie's ideal surrogate father, but he is also his closest friend. As the Scottish villagers sit huddled in a bomb shelter during a German air raid, Jamie, unperturbed by the noises from above, appears contented and entirely preoccupied with acquiring another child's apple. Although this scene establishes his lack of fear during an event which, collectively, is experienced as terrifying, it also establishes the significance of apples as a recurring motif in the *Trilogy*. During their initial meetings, for example, Jamie teaches Helmuth English with the help of a schoolbook. '"A" is for apple' is the first lesson in the book, and Jamie's subsequent yearnings for apples clearly translate into his longing for Helmuth and for the father and home he represents.[6] And while for the villagers the end of the war is cause for celebration and, as such, an event sure to become a positive part of their collective memories, for Jamie, this national victory signals a personal loss: Helmuth is sent home.

Thus, images of communal rejoicing are followed by images of Jamie's rapid descent into depression. Likewise, the emotions generated by another national conflict, the Suez Crisis, also fail to reflect Jamie's own, and provide further evidence of the incompatibility of Douglas's personal experiences with national imperatives. While the events of the mid-1950s spawned much tension and caused major divisions in Britain, Jamie's tenure in Egypt during this period is characterised by an unyielding boredom. Indeed, time appears to stand still as he and Robert search for ways of alleviating the monotony. Often at a loss for what to do, they alternately sit or stand around outside the barracks, and perform menial tasks such as painting bricks or smoothing out the sand, tasks which only serve to exacerbate their listlessness. Never once does the film show any hint of conflict and, for example, during a trip to the city, it is made clear that Jamie feels a close affinity with members of the local population.

Helmuth's third function in the narrative, as a soldier denied the possibility of returning to his home, is to provide an image of exile. In fact, Helmuth is doubly exiled, in that he is always physically separated from the other POWs for whom he is frequently an object of ridicule. In this, his experience mirrors Jamie's own: they are kindred spirits excluded both from their respective communities and from the particular groups to which they most naturally seem to belong. This parallel, of course, is to be expected, given that Helmuth is Jamie's invention. The rather unlikely pairing of a poor Scottish child and a middle-aged German soldier also suggests that for Douglas the concept of home in not contingent on place, but rather is made possible only through shared emotional experiences in time; experiences which in turn facilitate shared memories. This idea is further reinforced by Douglas's decision to film scenes between Helmuth and Jamie outdoors in large open spaces, in stark contrast to the claustrophobic houses and flats which are the structures conventionally understood as home. Windswept fields and empty sky filmed from a low angle accentuate the vastness of the space that surrounds the characters, while scenes filmed indoors are often shot from a high angle to emphasise the smallness of the room. Interestingly, Helmuth prefigures the sense of home as belonging that Jamie finally finds when he meets Robert. Although Jamie's relationship with Helmuth is necessarily different from his relationship with Robert (in that Helmuth is a paternalistic figure, and Robert features more as a friend), there are clear

parallels: encounters with both men are set against a backdrop of vast open spaces (the desert, in Robert's case); both
teach, guide, and nurture Jamie; and both, though of their
own choice, are positioned always outside the group. Robert's
exclusion, like Jamie's, is established in a visually striking scene:
a group of soldiers are gathered in a tight circle preparing to
set a spider on fire. Robert is off to the side, reading. At first,
Jamie ventures over to the group, but just before the crucial
moment when the creature is set ablaze, he leaves to join
Robert.

Setting a helpless insect on fire is perhaps a common, albeit
disturbing, ritual of childhood, but just as Jamie is unable to
share the prevailing emotions triggered by collective events, so
too he does not participate in rituals of any kind, whether
childhood, national or general cultural rituals, and this is
another recurring theme that enables Douglas to represent
Jamie's exclusion from group activities and spaces and consequently from group memories. Jamie's marginalisation from
national rituals is highlighted at various points in the *Trilogy*.
Towards the end of Part Two, for instance, an image of the
National Monument on Calton Hill appears on the screen, in
a shot lasting seven seconds. The function of this image is to
provide a conceptual filter through which to read the following shot: Jamie crossing paths with kilted pipers playing 'Scotland the Brave' as he makes his way to the children's home.
The Monument, a 'ruin' modelled on the Parthenon and
erected in the nineteenth century, is linked to the pipers
through their common role as signifiers of official Scottish culture. Yet, as a relic of Greek antiquity, the National Monument
is a fake. Its presence betrays an attempt to imbue the construct of Scottishness with the virtues of a foreign and distant
(and mythologised) past. This inflects our perception of that
with which it is allied: the subsequent display of tartanry. That
we should question the authenticity of the tradition symbol-
ised by the kilt and bagpipes as well as its inability to reflect
Jamie's reality is also suggested visually by the fact that Jamie
and the pipers are travelling in opposition directions. Part
Three opens with a similarly scathing commentary on tradition, and one, moreover, which also manages to bridge *My Ain
Folk* and *My Way Home*. Jamie, dressed in a kilt and a crisp white
shirt, is waiting for the cue to present a bouquet of flowers to the
Provost of the children's home and his family. Standing still, he
looks the model of Scottishness, but when he begins to walk
across the room (and thus in effect comes to life) his trouser

legs, rolled up underneath his kilt, begin to unfurl and cause him to stop short (see Hobsbawm and Ranger 1983).

Although, in this instance, Jamie appears powerless against an unseen determinism that prevents even his symbolic admittance to a group, he later takes active measures to reject the attempts made by other people to encourage him to don the uniforms that signal belonging to particular social strata. Following a tailor's comments that he 'looks like a gentleman' in a suit far too large for him, Jamie immediately visits a public washroom, leaving the suit behind there, and as he emerges in his own clothing, we see him walking past the sign that reads 'Gentlemen'. On another occasion, when the cruelty of Granny Douglas becomes unbearable, he relies on a Scottish myth learnt in school that placing a certain flower under someone's bed will lead to their death. However, not only does this spell fail to work on Granny Douglas but to make matters worse, the very next day, Grandfather Douglas returns home from the hospital. Although the irony pervading such moments provides an odd sort of comic relief, the scenes in question nevertheless point to the potential for exclusion operated by seemingly innocuous rituals.

In the following section of this essay, I shall focus on one particular scene that engages openly with the idea of ritual in order to identify ways in which its composition deliberately prevents narrative understanding, thus creating an experience of exclusion for the viewer. In the first shot, the viewer is confronted with an image of Tommy standing over his mother's grave upon which a bunch of poppies has been carefully placed. In the following shot, these same poppies are seen indoors, arranged in a teacup; Tommy has brought them home for his grandmother. Next, we see Jamie throw the poppies onto the floor and pour boiling water into the teacup until it overflows. He then casts out the water, carries the empty cup over to his grandmother, unfolds her fingers, and presses the warm cup into her hands. This scene is, in many ways, quite remarkable, for it demonstrates the incompatibility of ostensibly appropriate cultural ritual with current needs. The gift of flowers, however thoughtful, is not able to warm the old woman's hands, and in these terms the child's actions are entirely rational. Yet, this scene, like a number of others in the film, actually forces the spectators to feel excluded through its formal distanciation strategies. While such strategies frequently function in the *Trilogy* to align the audience with Jamie's experience, for example, rendering adult conversation inaudible, this scene is more complex.[7] It unfolds in a manner that prohibits us from making sense of it until the action is complete and we have had a moment to contemplate its significance. The sequence of events has a montage quality; stationary shots document each successive action quite candidly and objectively. We are forced to experience this moment as a child might experience the world: without explanation or sense of context or cause and effect. In other words, no concessions help the viewer negotiate this scene and what is, with hindsight, a poignant moment is actually rather difficult to watch.

In *Landscape for a Good Woman*, an autobiographical project which is, in a number of ways similar to that of Bill Douglas, Carolyn Steedman writes that 'children do not possess a social analysis of what is happening to them, or around them, so the landscape and the pictures it presents have to remain a background, taking on meaning later, from different circumstances' (Steedman 1986: 28). Although viewing Jamie's action as an isolated fragment of memory conveys the uncritical perspective of a child, this scene's juxtaposition with the image of Tommy at his mother's grave betrays the presence of the present in defining the significance of past events. While in terms of narrative content this scene is from the perspective of a child, visually it is from the perspective of an adult (indicated by such techniques as the steep downward angle of the camera, for example), and thus the dual vision of autobiography does much to complicate narrative focalisation. In this instance, Douglas recreates the moment that signalled the start of Tommy's participation in cultural rituals. The scene also signals Jamie's missed, and never quite regained, opportunity to be a part of (and thus benefit from) the community that such participation promises, including the possibility of a sense of belonging to a greater history.

Indeed, this sense of belonging was something Douglas himself never really seemed to be able to enjoy. His attempt to represent his memories and to articulate his experience of exile cinematically led to further exclusions. Despite winning countless awards, the *Trilogy* has received relatively little attention from cultural and political arenas as well as from academia. Scottish heritage interests, in particular, have rejected the film for its negative portrayal of Scottish life and the Scottish past and, as Caughie laments, by not offering commercially viable images for an English-language market, the *Trilogy* 'failed to meet the primary requirement of British film investment' (Dick, Noble and Petrie 1993: 197). It is not that these particular groups found Douglas's work thematically irrelevant but rather, as Andrew O'Hagan explains, that while 'home' is a common and recurring theme in Scottish art, literature and cinema, the way in which Douglas chose to address this topic 'put him strangely out of step with prevailing intellectual modes and practices in his native country' (Dick, Noble and Petrie 1993: 213–15). While cold economic logic, however deplorable (and, I think, specious, for reasons too numerous to address here) might easily explain such attitudes, the fact that Marxist film criticism was the intellectual mode that both rejected and ignored the *Trilogy* is, on the other hand, a more puzzling phenomenon. Some critics, such as Caughie, have suggested that Marxist neglect of Douglas's work is partly due to their engagement, at the time, with an avant-garde formalism that categorised the *Trilogy*'s 'humanist realism' as individualistic. This failure, he assures us, has resulted in the subsequent necessary expressions of guilt (Dick, Noble and Petrie 1993: 197). Andrew Noble suggests that Scottish theoretical Marxists may well have objected, in particular, to the fact that Jamie is saved by Robert who is both upper class and English (Dick, Noble and Petrie 1993: 153). Additionally, we might also point to the absence of the visual and literary iconography of working class life: the diligent miner, the saintly mother, and the sense of community embodied and engendered by the Working Man's Club.[8] For example: Jamie's father, a miner, is selfish, lazy and immature; both grandmothers, as mother figures, fail to nurture and protect the boys; and, community is achieved only for some at the expense of others. However, rather than undermine the dignity of working class life or denigrate the positive images that play a crucial role in its representations, Douglas's *Trilogy*, in challenging its stereotypes, has added a much needed depth. And significantly, as Joyce McMillan argues, this includes a challenge to the stereotypical representations of working class women. She explains that contrary to the saintly and improbable one-dimensionality of the dominant Hoggartian mother figure, Douglas's grandmothers 'are not benign, passive, self-abnegating figures, but human beings, women with passions, needs and desires; and that where these are repressed and thwarted, violence and cruelty, will result, as surely as in men' (Dick, Noble and Petrie 1993: 222). Thus, Douglas draws attention to the complex matrix of working class identities, showing that each deserves representation and a place in working class histories.

Aesthetically a blend of the realist and European art cinema traditions, and narratively a deeply personal exploration of memory and exile, the *Trilogy* did not satisfy enough of the criteria needed to enlist the support of the Scottish establishment, British funding bodies or Marxist film criticism. This however does not mean that it did not speak to a wider audience. Although the *Trilogy* is, quite simply, an intensely moving and brilliant work, it somehow failed to be emblematic in the ways required by those entrusted with the power to legitimate it at the particular cultural moment of its production. Douglas did not set out to challenge the tenets of the institutions and paradigms that rejected him. His concern, first and foremost, was the presentation of his memories in a way that would touch the emotional and intellectual sensibilities of his audience. Yet, in retrospect (and in part thanks to the developments in our understanding of history and memory) we might consider how the *Trilogy*, in refusing to become emblematic for a particular historical discourse, exists as a text that effectively and usefully complicates and thereby enriches, among other things, representations of working class life. Steedman comments on the need to illustrate what she calls 'lives lived out on the borderlands', those living in exile from the communities of which they are physically a part yet to which they do not belong (Steedman 1986: 5). Like Douglas, she too found that 'personal observations of past time – the stories that people tell themselves in order to explain how they got to the place they inhabit – are often in deep and ambiguous conflict with the official interpretative devices of a culture' (Steedman 1986: 6). Particularity and detail are important, not simply to illuminate historical understanding, but to prevent the ways in which some historical discourses exclude by summarising and generalising the past. Perhaps this is what we should highlight as a crucial role for those autobiographies crafted with integrity and which not only seek to portray what is personally remembered, but also to question how we remember, what is the function of memory, and how we share our memories with others.

Mamoun Hassan, head of production at the British Film Institute and one of the few champions of Douglas's cause, describes the *Trilogy* as 'an act of revenge' presumably against those responsible for his childhood suffering (Dick, Noble and Petrie 1993: 149–150). However, we might also look at the film as an act of revenge against community and history in general. Douglas lays bare the mechanisms and strategies by which a community, in defining the limits of inclusion, can exclude not only from its spaces and practices, but also from the memories and histories that result from shared experience. Although the *Trilogy* documents a search for home and thus suggests a desire for belonging, its simultaneous condemnation of community clearly exposes the paradoxes and dilemmas that plague such quests. Its complex nature provides us with an opportunity to explore the intricacies and the functions of memory in attempting a cinematic inscription into history of personal experiences, and thereby to expand both our conception of history and of what constitutes a meaningful engagement with the past.

Notes

1. I would like to thank Wendy Everett and Laura Mulvey for their helpful comments on an earlier version of this essay.
2. Here, 'history' is understood as the work of traditional professional historians concerned with the events and leaders of a nation, and 'memory' as the personal memories of an individual. (However, according to Raphael Samuel, Douglas's *Trilogy* can be considered 'history' since 'history is not the prerogative of the historian... [but] rather, a social form of knowledge; the work, in any given instance, of a thousand different hands' (Samuel 1994, 8). Memory, he claims, whose modes of transmission may be written, oral or visual is 'dialectically related' to history, and is itself 'historically conditioned' (Samuel 1994, x). Collective memory, the shared memories and experiences of a community or a particular social group, also plays a role in the *Trilogy*. However, just as personal memory need not necessarily coincide with the collective memories of a specific group, so too those collective memories may differ from the official version of history. In the *Trilogy*, one of Douglas's primary concerns is the irreconcilability of personal memory with both collective memory and history.
3. This reference to photography alludes to the photograph's intimate connection with memory. Interestingly, in *Distant Voices, Still Lives*, Terence Davies (whose work is often seen in relation to the Douglas *Trilogy*) composes shots that closely resemble the photographs commonly found in family albums.
4. There are exceptions to this which complicate point of view in the film. On occasion, the visual and psychological perspective shifts to Douglas the adult recounting the past from the vantage of the present. As a result, diegetic focalisation shifts to narration. One important example is the tea cup scene which is discussed in more detail later in the essay.
5. Helmuth personifies Jamie's yearning and is thus, in some ways, an object of nostalgia. However, although nostalgia is tied to memory and history, detailing how the *Trilogy* engages with nostalgia or might itself be nostalgic, is beyond the scope of this paper.
6. In fact, the words used to illustrate the letters of the alphabet may all be seen as significant, and as prefiguring important moments in the *Trilogy*: 'B'

stands for boy and thus Jamie; 'C' for cat, and for Jamie's pet which meets
an untimely end at the hands of Tommy; 'D' for dog and the whippet trea-
sured by Granny Douglas which alternately provides a scapegoat and
receives attention at Jamie's expense.

7. It is important to note that the conversations that Jamie is unable to hear
tend to have a direct impact upon his life, again signalling his overall lack
of control. One such, between the headmaster at the children's home and
his father, presumably concerns his temporary return to Granny Douglas's,
while another between the same headmaster and a prospective foster
mother, precedes a very brief and unsuccessful placement.

8. These archetypal figures, documented by Richard Hoggart in *The Uses of
Literacy* 1957 (London: Penguin, 1992), have found expression countless
times in literature, film and television. Powerful and relatively recent
examples might include the much-derided final plays of Dennis Potter,
Karaoke and *Cold Lazarus* (1996). Here, the quintessential images of postwar
British working class life are, through various formal and narrative strategies, framed as real and authentic and thus deserving of preservation and
commemoration.

References

Buck-Morss, S. (1994) 'The Cinema as Prosthesis of Perception:
A Historical Account', in Seremetakis, N. (ed.), *The Senses Still:
Perception and Memory as Material Culture in Modernity*, Boulder:
Westview Press, 45–62.

Dick, E., A. Noble and D. Petrie (eds) (1993) *Bill Douglas: A
Lanternist's Account*, London: British Film Institute.

Elsaesser, T. (1999) '"One train may be hiding another": private
history, memory and national identity', *Screening the Past* 6
(July 1999): 19 paragraphs. 9 Mar. 2000 [www.latrobe.
edu.au/screeningthepast/reruns/rr0499/terr6b.htm].

Hobsbawm, E. and T. Ranger (eds) (1983) *The Invention of Tradition*,
Cambridge: Cambridge University Press.

Huyssen, A. (1995) *Twilight Memories: Marking Time in a Culture of
Amnesia*, London: Routledge.

LaCapra, D. (1985) *History and Criticism*, London: Cornell University
Press.

Monk, C. and A. Sargeant (eds) (2002) *British Historical Cinema*,
London: Routledge.

Radstone, S. (1995) 'Cinema/Memory/History', *Screen* (36)1 (Spring),
34–47.

Samuel, R. (1994) *Theatres of Memory*, London: Verso.

Steedman, C. (1986) *Landscape for a Good Woman*, London: Virago.

White, H. (1973) *Metahistory: The Historical Imagination in
Nineteenth-Century Europe*, London: The Johns Hopkins
University Press.

Yates, F. (1996) *The Art of Memory*, Harmondsworth: Penguin.

PART III

BODY

CHAPTER 8

EXILE AND THE BODY

Gabriele Griffin

This chapter focuses on the somatic experiences associated with exile and their relation to cognition. The evidence it draws upon is cultural and encompasses theatre work, visual imagery, autobiographical writings, and other forms of cultural representation. Underlying that use is the understanding that there is a relation between the actual, material experiences of exile and their representation in culture and that, however contested that relationship might be, it must not be obliterated. The reason for this lies in the meaning(s) of exile.

Exile is not a singular condition. The compact edition (1979) of the *Oxford English Dictionary* has four major entries for 'exile' which include, as its meaning, 'state of banishment, devastation, destruction', 'one compelled to reside away from his native land', 'to banish, to ravage'. The vocabulary articulating 'exile' emphasises the notion of force, of forced evacuation, but also of deliberate destruction, ravishment and devastation. Exile is thus always the effect of force exerted upon a person or a people, resulting in a condition which is not freely chosen but inflicted, an experience where the subjecthood of the individual is called into question as s/he becomes the object of a displacing power which s/he is unable to resist. The experience of exile produces cultural expressions of that condition, both by those who have actually undergone or been in a state of exile, and by those affected by the exile they observe or experience indirectly.

In contemporary culture, exile is an inescapable phenomenon. Everyday via the news media we observe exile as it occurs, literally while we are watching. The forced displacement of people as they flee war zones, droughts, famines, natural catastrophes such as volcanic eruptions or earthquakes, or economic devastation has become part of our daily cultural diet to the extent that, particularly from the Gulf War onwards, a body of critical literature has emerged which – drawing particularly on the work of Hannah Arendt – has begun to ask questions about how to understand the seemingly growing indifference of the viewing public to events which exile and devastate whole peoples right in front of our eyes without resulting in any very significant reactions. It is within this context, the visibility of exile to us on the one hand, and the seeming indifference to it many manifest on the other, that I locate my discussion of exile and my assertion that it is important to remember the relationship between the actual lived experience of exile and its rendition or representation in culture. I want to suggest that exile is not a de-materialised condition but that it has somatic realities that we need to consider and engage with.

For me exile is about pain, about physical and psychical pain, about a somatically enacted process whereby subjugated subjectivities are fashioned and sustained. In this chapter I shall briefly discuss five examples of how this occurs. They are:

1. the representations of the atrocities, the rape and torture committed in Bosnia as part of the ethnic wars there, and by extension, the use of torture as part of a political strategy of domination;
2. the impact of sexual abuse in non-war settings on its victims;
3. the female body constructed as decorative and commodified, in perpetual need of correction, modification, improvement as evidenced through the advertising and popular cultural industries in late capitalist societies, and as critiqued by artists such as Orlan (1996),[1] for example;
4. the representation of the impact of HIV/AIDS on bodies (see Crimp 1991, Watney 1994, Patton 1996, Griffin 2000); and finally,
5. the impact of the experience of racism on racialised bodies.

Following discussions of each of these I shall make some general comments about conceptions of the body in contemporary theory and their relation to the issue of exile and the body.

Atrocities in War

In December 2000 the Young Vic Theatre in London put on a play by the Romanian playwright Matei Visniec entitled *The Body of a Woman as a Battlefield in the Bosnian War.* The play deals with the impact of the ethnically motivated gang rape of a woman as she is treated, in the aftermath of the war, in a clinic in Germany. It articulates the traumatised, alienated psychic condition the woman endures as the consequence of the somatic injuries she has suffered. The abuse, rape, and torture of women, the refiguring of their bodies as battlefields, in a context where the United Nations have declared bodily integrity as a human right, resulted in 2000 at the International War Crimes Tribunal in the Hague in the declaration of rape as a war crime – the first time ever this was achieved.[2] But such legal interventions mean relatively little to those who live the long-term somatic consequences of the actual violation. In the play, for example, Dorra, the Bosnian woman, is pregnant as a consequence of the rape. She does not want the child and, in actuality, many of the women who were raped during the war and were made pregnant as a result of rape either aborted or attempted to abort, often with further serious consequences for their health, or committed suicide, rather than bear the shame and degradation of carrying an unwanted child. In the play Dorra's body continues to be a battleground even after she has been removed from the geographical site of the battle, as Kate, an American clinical psychologist, herself suffering from post-traumatic stress as a consequence of having participated in the excavation of mass graves, attempts to persuade Dorra first not to abort, and then to give her the child. For Kate, Dorra's body has become synonymous with the mass graves she helped excavate. As she loses patience with Dorra's resistance, she says:

> Your belly is a mass grave, Dorra. When I think of your belly, I see a pit full of corpses, dried up, or swollen, or rotting... And, in this mass of corpses, there's something moving... A human being... Amongst all these dead, there's someone left alive... asking to be gotten out of there... I'll never let you kill this child, Dorra. I came to your country to learn how to open up mass graves. And each time I opened one, I did it with the irrational hope that there'd be just one survivor... This child is a survivor, Dorra. And it must be saved – to be pulled out of there. There... It's as simple as that... It must be pulled out of that mass grave... (Visniec 2000: 58)

The complete disregard of Dorra as a person here, her somatisation, instrumentalisation and territorialisation effected in the name of saving the psychologist from her own horror, bespeaks the objectified condition the exiled person is made to endure. In *The Body of a Woman as a Battlefield in the Bosnian War* and, indeed, whenever people flee war-torn zones or dictatorial regimes, the body becomes both the ground for their exile and the source which legitimates their exile. The ability to show a body in pieces, a traumatised, wounded, visibly tortured body is the means by which the condition of exile becomes legitimated and asylum is granted. This sets the parameters for how forced dispossession is rendered the cause for refugee status. You may remember the horrendous descriptions of bodily violation, of torture and abuse which Rigoberta Menchú (1984) described as part of her narrative representation of her life as a Guatemalen peasant and resistance fighter.[3] In many ways, her biography is a biography of the body – the body as a battlefield. Whilst Menchú describes the body at the point of violation, albeit retrospectively, Visniec's play is about the fate of the body after it has been violated, when the person whose body has been violated is in exile – in exile both from her country and from her body. Initially silent, Dorra is eventually able to articulate her hatred of the child within her and of the country which she associates with her own violation. Her ability to talk functions as the beginning of her reintegration into her bodily self, her repossession of her dispossessed body, her attempt to overcome her exile from her own body.

In Timberlake Wertenbaker's play *Credible Witness*, shown at the Royal Court Theatre in London in February 2001, and set in a detention centre for asylum seekers in the United Kingdom, Ameena, the refugee who has also been the object of rape in her war-torn country, is unable to speak about what was done to her, in fact, unable to cope with any direct interaction, and is on the brink of having her request for asylum refused because she cannot, metadiscursively, turn her body into the body of evidence required to secure the necessary proof of her violation. Her silence measures the extent to which her violation has trapped her in her body, has made it impossible for her to enact the notion of 'mind over matter' – mind is matter here, mind has been melted into matter as violation reduces the distance between mind and matter, between body and consciousness to the point where only the body exists. This is why, at the Medical Foundation for the Victims of Torture, established by Helen Bamber in north London in 1985, 'everything starts with the body':

> Bamber and her physicians have become expert in the effects of torture: soft tissue damage to muscles and lignaments from beating with sticks and rifle butts, on the trunk, or the soles of the feet; and damage to the lumbar region, which hurts not only the back, but also the legs. Painful shoulder joints because of 'Palestinian hanging', in which the victim is suspended from a rope by his arms tied behind his back; eye injuries, such as degeneration of the optic nerve, so that vision blurs; and many epilepsies, which are caused by blows to the head (Belton 1999: 2).

The foundation works to effect a reconciliation between body and mind, corporeality and subjectivity, to counteract the meltdown which torture has brought about.

Seamus Heaney's poem about the archer Philoctetes who betrayed Odysseus, describes 'people no one will cure or rescue', those exiled beyond redemption or recovery:

> Nothing there except
> The beat of the waves and the beat of my raw
> wound...
> I managed to come through
> But I never healed.
> My whole life has been
> Just one long cruel parody (Heaney 1990)

That beat of the waves, the interminable affliction, is visually enacted in a work by the artist and academic Mary Kelly, entitled *Mea Culpa* (1999), which was on show at the Robert Sandelson Gallery in London in spring 2001. Here, on waves of grey lint, compressed fragments of fibre from a domestic tumble dryer, are descriptions of 'politically motivated' atrocities committed in the last three decades which have been the objects of investigations by the International War Crimes Tribunal in The Hague. Each set of grey lint waves carries a single line of continuous text referring to one major site of such atrocities, from Phnom Pehn, to Beirut, Buenos Aires, and Johannesburg. As the 2000 Report by Amnesty International, part of their 'Stamp Out Torture' campaign, stated: 'Worldwide torture on the rise'. The abstraction of that statement belies the reality of the experience of that abuse by each individual who is the object of it. It points to the ubiquity of it but, and this is where Kelly's work is salutary in its specificity, it does not and cannot give an account of the meaning of that experience for the individual who suffers it. 'I managed to come through/but I never healed' – that is the tenor of the actual embodied, lived experience of those who have been tortured and raped. The number of suicides and the experience of ultimate destitution among exiled peoples is very high indeed. One graphic account of this is provided by the Cuban author Reinaldo Arenas who led a nomadic existence following his exile from Cuba and in 1990 committed suicide in New York. His biography, *Before Night Falls*, offers a chilling account of the impact of abuse and exile on those who experience it. 'I managed to come through/but I never healed' might well be their refrain.

The Impact of Sexual Abuse in Non-War Settings on its Victims

It is also the refrain of women and children who are the victims of sexual abuse in non-war settings. Some years ago I worked with a social worker who dealt with families in which sexual abuse had occurred and specifically with the mothers in those families. Simultaneously I had a friend who fostered sexually abused young girls – one of the conditions of fostering such children being that they are placed in all-female households. What I learnt from those experiences, and from reading about sexual abuse, is that in cases of sustained and severe sexual abuse a child will switch off when the abuse occurs, go into a state of dissociation or fugue where the mind becomes dissociated from the body so that what is happening to the body is not allowed to filter into the mind. It is an attempt to prevent the kind of meltdown described above. It is a kind of triumph of mind over matter, an attempt to keep intact the mind when matter – and therefore mind – is at risk. The long-term use of this coping strategy, the desperate attempt to retain an inviolate part of yourself, is that the child loses control over the process of switching into and out of this fugue state, that it begins to happen all the time, involuntarily. A different kind of meltdown sets in. Part of the post-traumatic, therapeutic effort is to help the child regain control, re-establish the ability to choose a state of connectedness to the body and to a certain kind of material reality that she wants. Part of such girls' own, often hidden, strategies of attempting to regain a connection to the body is to self-harm through cutting the body, giving oneself a momentary intense bodily experience of one's own making. 'I managed to come through/But I never healed' is the refrain of those girls, becoming women, actual women as the body remains, for many, the site of a perpetual battle for control, *their* control, a continuously contested terrain from which they have been forcibly exiled and to which they find it virtually impossible to return.[4]

The Female Body as a Paradigmatic Site of Exile

That state of permanent exile, of continued, forcible eviction, resulting in the objectification of the body into the abject (see Kristeva 1982), of a dissociation of body from mind in which the mind does continuous battle with the body in an effort to control it on behalf of hegemonic discourses of female decorativity, is the condition which fashions women's lives in western and many other cultures. Paula Weidegger's highly influential book *History's Mistress* (1986) testifies to the anthropo-historical dimension of this phenomenon, as do sites such as the Musée de L'Homme in Paris and elsewhere which detail the history of body modification that women have been the objects of and participated in, in the service of certain normativities of femininity which circulate in most cultures and act as structures of regulation and containment of the abjected female body (see Bordo 1993). This is the process by which, as a function of the powers of horror which pertain to this abjected state, lead us to become, as Kristeva has put it, 'strangers to ourselves.' Many of the practices involved evacuate women from their bodies, require them literally to 'take leave of their senses', not to feel, not to hear, not to see, not to speak, in order to approximate, yet never be equal to, the ideals of femininity to which they become subjugated. Conventional women's magazines conventionally produce, as part of the logic of late capitalism (see Falk 1994), an image of women as persistently lacking (see Ferguson 1983 and Winship 1987), perpetually in need of modification and improvement, responsible individually both for their lack and for implementing a rescue plan which, in next month's or next week's issue, will only see them exiled again, as the boundaries shift, and territory gained is lost again, almost immediately. One might be tempted to argue that the female body is the paradigmatic site of exile, embodies the exilic condition par excellence. But the pervasiveness of its condition, its ubiquity also acts as the meliorating factor which normalises this condition, enabling texts such Helen Fielding's *Bridget Jones' Diary* to become bestsellers through the recognition they activate in subjugated female subjectivities, recognition – but not resistance.

The Representation of the Impact of HIV/AIDS on Bodies

In contrast, both recognition and resistance have characterised the responses by those who have suffered from HIV/AIDS, either directly through becoming infected or indirectly through being involved, on some level, with those suffering from HIV/AIDS.[5] When we talk about HIV/AIDS and the body, the bodies we are actually referring to belong to those already exiled culturally, politically, socially, and economically (see Chirimuuta and Chirimuuta 1987, Phelan 1997). The largest groups of people with HIV/AIDS in the world today are people from the so-called third world, Africa and Asia, and gay men and drug users in the western world. Where we are looking at the third world, we are looking at bodies economically exploited, frequently living in countries that are either in states of transition or that are war-torn, where the disenfranchisement of the individual assumes dimensions we cannot even begin to imagine. The exile experienced here is not the exile of a geographical remove from a space one might call home but an exile imposed from without and experienced from within in a position of stasis dominated by the unchecked, or virtually unchecked, proliferation of the virus and of infection. Only in 2001 did the pharmaceutical companies finally agree to allow cheaper drugs to combat the HIV virus and infection to be distributed in the so-called third world countries. But even with that, there is still the issue of treatment regimes that involve the taking of between twenty and thirty tablets per day with the attendant necessity of fresh water and refrigeration that is almost impossible to come by in some parts of the world.

Unlike the female acquiescence into an exilic condition of abjected femininity – a condition which is, of course, in that instance not usually life-threatening – HIV/AIDS activists around the world, and especially from within the various gay communities, have fought very hard and, as the victory over the pharmaceutical companies shows, very effectively, against the exilic condition which threatened many – but not just – gay men's lives with the advent of AIDS. The strong sense of just being left to die which informed gay men's perception of the lack of intervention in the disease from western govern-ments when it first became apparent, led to sustained cam-paigns to combat governmental apathy, justified by the notion that those affected were already othered communities whose access to resources was – as a function of their very oth-erness – always already, as the phrase goes, a matter of sociopolitical contestation. In this context, helping, curing, 'saving' becomes part of an economy that operates to contest the exclusion endured by those excluded, bringing them back into a fold that undoes the exilic condition. In an effort to counteract the exilic condition generated by the notion that HIV/AIDS was a gay disease, the Health Education Authority in the United Kingdom ran a series of campaigns designed to emphasise that HIV/AIDS could happen to anyone (Field, Wellings and McVey: 1997). One of their poster campaigns, for example, stated: 'If AIDS only affects 0.002% of the popula-tion why is this advertisement appearing in every national daily newspaper?' (1988–9). In *Strangers to Ourselves* Julia Kristeva (1991) has analysed the ways in which the otherness of others maintains the selfsameness of those who do the othering. She asks: 'are we not speaking beings only if we dis-tinguish ourselves from others in order to impart to them our personal meaning on the basis of such a perceived and assumed difference?' (Kristeva 1991: 41–2). Kristeva's inten-tion is to argue for a reconciliation between self and other, a recognition of the strangeness that resides both within the self and the other as the precondition of a situation where 'A para-doxical community is emerging, made up of foreigners who are reconciled with themselves to the extent that they recog-nise themselves as foreigners'. (Kristeva 1991: 195). But this is not the state in which we live, and it is precisely for this reason that attempts to undo the exilic condition of those suffering from HIV/AIDS were, and in some respects continue to be, so vigorously contested by certain kinds of hegemonic discourses and institutions.

The Impact of the Experience of Racism on Racialised Bodies

Whilst the exilic condition activated through HIV/AIDS is in some respects a secondary condition to an already established one of exclusion based, in the case of gay men, on sexual identity, the exilic condition effected through racism is premised on perceptions of physical difference which fuel and maintain another kind of xenophobia. Hannah Höch's collage of 1970 entitled 'Angst' or 'Fear' is extremely telling here (Museen der Stadt Gotha 1993). It is a portrait, focusing on the head and shoulders, and featuring a black-skinned androgynous figure whose chief facial traits serve to signal the embodiment of a black other. Fear, in this image, is black, has bulging eyes, an outsize thick-lipped mouth which is bright orange-red and functions as the visual centre of the image, and is expressive both of a terror within and a terror without.[6] The image could signify the fear a black person might feel when confronted with a lynch mob, or it could be the incarnation of fear as it might be embodied for/by the viewer. The collage plays on both an ambiguity concerning the location of fear (is it in 'us' or is it 'them'?) and on its ubiquity (we, the viewers might feel that fear, or think of fear in those terms, and the person depicted might feel that fear – it is within us and outside of us, within the other and embodied by the other). One might argue that the collage drives towards the position on 'strangeness' or the foreign articulated in Kristeva's work on the topic, namely that it drives towards an understanding of foreignness being something inherent in ourselves as much as being something attributable to others. However, that recognition is far from achieved in contemporary society. Othering still leads to abjection, and the calling into question of the (self)-worth of those othered through racism demands that the racialised exile view herself as an object of interrogation in which her psychical self, her somatic self, and the racism the latter is the object of, are brought into some form of alignment, if not reconciliation. This is what Adrian Piper, artist and academic, writes about this condition in 'Xenophobia and the Indexical Present':

> My experiences as a third-world woman in mainstream society have been strongly influenced by attempts to marginalise or ostracise me, both socially and professionally, from the mainstream; or, at the very least, to put me in my (subordinate) place in it ... My strategy of self-defense is to transform pain into meaning (Piper 1996: 245).

Here is a version of the pain I referred to at the beginning of this chapter when I wrote that 'For me exile is about pain, about physical and psychical pain, about a somatically-enacted process whereby subjugated subjectivities are fashioned and sustained.' Piper may be able to convert her pain into meaning and come through as well as heal, but in Toni Morrison's *The Bluest Eye* (1970), Pecola, the little black girl who is forcibly exiled from her body because of the meaning imposed on its blackness, is unable to come through and heal. Initially hating those who hate her, she eventually internalises the xenophobia which characterises their attitude, thus becoming utterly subjugated. This is what happens:

> I destroyed white baby dolls. But the dismembering of dolls was not the true horror. The truly horrifying thing was the transference of the same impulses to little white girls. The indifference with which I could have axed them was shaken only by my desire to do so... When I learned how repulsive this disinterested violence was, that it was repulsive because it was disinterested, my shame floundered about for a refuge. The best hiding place was love. Thus the conversion from pristine sadism to fabricated hatred, to fraudulent love. It was a small step to Shirley Temple. I learned much later to worship her... (Morrison 1970: 24–25).

Pecola's worship of Shirley Temple, which ultimately results in Pecola's psychic self-destruction since it is only through that process that she is able to approximate Temple, in some respects resembles Michael Jackson's surgical attempts at his own somatic transformation into Elizabeth Taylor.[7] Here we have the figure of the exile who not so much mourns the loss as the impossibility of becoming, whose fate is not to look backwards but forwards to an impossible and ultimately soul-if not body-destroying future. The desire to unmark, indeed to unmake, the exilic body becomes the raison d'être of those who have been forced to evacuate their somatic identities and for whom no healing semantics attaches to their somatic reality.

The Body in Theory

I want to make some closing remarks about the body in theory, and its relation to the exilic condition. It seems to me that at the beginning of the twenty-first century we have become very used to the notion of a denaturalised body upon which identities are inscribed. The literalisation of that is, of course, accomplished in Franz Kafka's novella *In the Penal Colony* (1914) in which the execution of the condemned man is supposed to be effected by the actual inscription of the punishment onto the condemned man's body. This somatisation of the judgment is in many respects the very opposite of what seems to me to be happening in current theories of the body in which a denaturalised physicality becomes abstracted to the extent that its unreality, its lack of material somatic substance, obliterates the very materiality it purports to address. In similar ways theorisations and representations of exile sometimes tend to evacuate the lived embodiment of that condition, except as a triumphalist narrative of overcoming. Both Michel Foucault's and Judith Butler's work on the body, for instance, are on one level a way of celebrating resistance, of suggesting opportunities for refusal in the interstices of regulatory regimes. Indeed, much writing on their work has tried to disentangle the extent to which subjects are always only subjects insofar as they are effected by regulatory regimes. There is nothing, as one might argue with Derrida, outside the text. However, the whole question of political intervention, and agency seems to demand, if we want to effect change, the possibility of regimes being shiftable, of change being able to occur. Somehow, somewhere, it must be possible to slip through the net. Bodies are materialities that are not mere objects in/as circulating discourses of power; they are embodied, lived realities which constitute and construct our subjectivities. They are not simply abstractions or prosthetic[8] – they are not unrelated to cognition. Triumphalist narratives of overcoming are the very opposite of Philoctetes' 'I managed to come through/but I never healed.' It is those who came through but never healed whom we need to attend to and whose exile as a condition of permanent estrangement we need to engage with.

Notes

1. Orlan's *ceci est mon corps... ceci est mon logiciel...* [*This is my body... this is my software...*], part of the documentation of a series of surgical interventions upon her body instigated by Orlan, provides an explanation of her critique of plastic surgery for the purpose of beautification. For a commentary on Orlan's frequently contested work see Augsburg 1998.
2. For details on these matters see the War Crimes Tribunal Watch website www.igc.apc.org/balkans/tribunal.html.

3. Menchú's writings have been the object of some subsequent critiques, rais-
   ing questions about the veracity of her account. See Stoll 1999.
4. The international journal *Child Abuse and Neglect* is a useful source on this
   topic.
5. One account of that resistance is detailed in Crimp's and Rolston's (1990)
   volume on the work of ACT UP, entitled *AIDSDEMOGRAPHICS*.
6. There is no space in this chapter to explore the symbolic significance of the
   mouth as the threshold between inner and outer but that significance is
   pertinent to the distinction between selfsame and other. Kristeva's *Powers of
   Horror* (1982) explores the idea of the mouth as one of the orifices which
   express the liminality of the body and contribute to the notion of the abject.
7. In 'Michael Jackson's Penis' (1995) Cynthia Fuchs analyses Jackson's various bodily transformations and their meanings. Offering a queer reading,
   Fuchs suggests that Jackson 'can only be an inexact copy of himself' (22)
   and that his perpetual estrangement from himself, embodied in his
   repeated transformations of that self, is difficult to interpret.
8. In *The War of Desire and Technology at the Close of the Mechanical Age* (the title
   itself is, of course, a reference to Walter Benjamin's famous work on art in
   the age of its reproducibility) Allucquère Rosanne Stone (better known to
   readers of queer theory as Sandy Stone) produces an extremely interesting
   analysis of the relationship between the actual material body and its tech-
   nologised representation. This analysis takes up the issue of the lived body
   and (political) agency in the context of encounters and constructions of
   subjectivity on the internet.

References

Arenas, R. (1993) *Before Night Falls: A Memoir*, translated by
   D. M. Koch, London: Penguin.
Augsburg, T. (1998) 'Orlan's Performative Transformations
   of Subjectivity', in Phelan, P., and J. Lane (eds), *The Ends
   of Performance*, New York: New York University Press, 285–314.
Belton, N. (1999) 'Helen versus Hell', *Guardian Unlimited*,
   10 January: 1–7 (www.guardian.co.uk/Archive/Article/
   0,4273,3805913,00.html).
Bordo, S. (1993) *Unbearable Weight: Feminism, Western Culture, and
   the Body*, Berkeley: University of California Press.
Chirimuuta, R. C. and R. J. Chirimuuta (1987) *Aids, Africa and
   Racism*. Stanhope, Derbyshire: Chirimuuta.
Crimp, D. (ed) (1991) *AIDS: Cultural Analysis, Cultural Activism*,
   Cambridge, MA: MIT Press.
Crimp, D. with A. Rolston (1990) *AIDSDEMOGRAPHICS*. Seattle:
   Bay Press.
Falk, P. (1994) *The Consuming Body*, London: Sage.
Ferguson, M. (1983) *Forever Feminine: Women's Magazines and
   the Cult of Femininity*, London: Heinemann Educational Books.
Field, B., K.Wellings and D. McVey (1997) *Promoting Safer Sex:
   A History of the Health Education Authority's Mass Media Campaigns*

on HIV, AIDS and Sexual Health 1987–1996, London: Health Education Authority.

Fielding, H. (1996) _Bridget Jones's Diary_, London: Picador.

Fuchs, C. J. (1995) 'Michael Jackson's Penis', in Case, S.-E., P. Brett, and S. Leigh Foster (eds), _Cruising the Performative_, Bloomington: Indiana University Press, 13–33.

Griffin, G. (2000) _Representations of HIV and AIDS: Visibility Blue/s_, Manchester: Manchester University Press.

Heaney, S. (1990) _The Cure At Troy: A Version of Sophocles' Philoctetes_, London: Faber and Faber, in conjunction with Field Day Theatre Co.

Kafka, F. (1914) 'In the Penal Colony,' reprinted in _Stories 1904–1924_, translated by J. A. Underwood, London: Macdonald and Co, 1981.

Kristeva, J. (1982) _Powers of Horror: An Essay on Abjection_, translated by Leon S. Roudiez, New York: Columbia University Press.

Kristeva, J. (1991) _Strangers to Ourselves_, London: Harvester Wheatsheaf.

Menchú, R. (1984) _I, Rigoberta Menchú: An Indian Woman in Guatemala_, London: Verso.

Morrison, T. (1970) _The Bluest Eye_, reprinted 1981, London: Triad/Panther.

Museen der Stadt Gotha (1993) _Hannah Höch: Gotha 1889–Berlin 1978_. Gotha: Museen der Stadt Gotha.

Orlan (1996) _Ceci est mon corps... ceci est mon logiciel..._ London: Black Dog Publishing.

Patton, C. (1996) _Fatal Advice_, Durham: Duke University Press.

Phelan, P. (1997) _Mourning Sex: Performing Public Memories_, London: Routledge.

Piper, A. (1996) _Out of Order, Out of Sight Vol. 1: Selected Writings in Meta-Art 1968–1992_, Cambridge, Mass.: MIT Press.

Stoll, D. (1999) _Rigoberta Menchú and the Story of All Poor Guatemalans_, Boulder, Colorado: Westview Press.

Stone, A. R. (1996) _The War of Desire and Technology at the Close of the Mechanical Age_, Cambridge, MA: MIT Press.

Visniec, M. (2000) _The Body of a Woman as a Battlefield in the Bosnian War_, in G. Landor and C. Robson (eds), _Balkan Plots: Plays from Central and Eastern Europe_, London: Aurora Metro Press, 14–62.

Watney, S. (1994) _Practices of Freedom: Selected Writings on HIV/AIDS_, London: Rivers Oram Press.

Weidegger, P. (1986) _History's Mistress: A New Interpretation of a 19th-century Ethnographic Classic_, Harmondsworth: Penguin.

Wertenbaker, T. (2001) _Credible Witness_, London: Faber and The Royal Court Theatre.

Winship, J. (1987) _Inside Women's Magazines_, London: Pandora.

CHAPTER 9

THE TRANSGENDERED INDIVIDUAL AS EXILIC TRAVELLING SUBJECT

Feroza Basu

In this article I consider the relationship between transgender, travel and exile as it emerges in a particular example of 1990s American literature, *Stone Butch Blues* by Leslie Feinberg. Generically, the work in question has been categorised variously as transgender fiction, fictionalised autobiography, and lesbian literature. It has not, to my knowledge, been classified as travel literature. However, throughout the text, the narrator specifically defines her collective experiences as constitutive of exile and a journey, so I have been interested in pursuing her interpretation of exile and travel as they relate to the circumstances she narrates, with a view to considering the implications for travel literature and travel theory. Exile will be considered symptomatically, in terms of contingent feelings of alienation; it will be considered conceptually in terms of separation from a notional 'home', and it will be considered from a causal point of view, in terms of its origin as coercive or non-coercive.

I am interested in possible conceptual overlap between travel variants and transsexuality. Some attention has already been given to this by critics working in various fields. Jan Morris's 1974 autobiography, *Conundrum: An Extraordinary Narrative of Transsexualism* is paradigmatic, being the autobiography of a transsexual travel writer. *Le Saut de L'Ange*, the 1987 autobiography of male-to-female transsexual Maud

Marin, does not focus on issues of geographical displacement, but Jean-Didier Urbain considers it in his theorisation of travel in *Secrets de Voyage* alongside accounts of travellers who have manipulated their physical appearance for the sake of travel. According to Urbain, such changes of appearance radically alter the nature of the traveller's interaction with other people, so that vertical travelling is achievable, in which the travel experience is not dependent upon actual displacement in geographical space. Urbain's treatment of this subject is problematic, however, as he overstates the case that boredom and curiosity are chief amongst the motivations of such travellers, some of whom have taken measures as drastic as amputation of body parts. There is no attempt to consider the role of gender dysphoria or physical danger incurred by contemporary subjects who already diverge from heterosocial norms of appearance or lifestyle.

Stone Butch Blues is announced as a work of fiction but, according to the preface, is intended to be an accurate illustration of actual lived experiences of gay and transgendered people. It was published in 1993 and covers the narrator's life from the 1950s to the 1980s. The section corresponding to the 1980s gives a very different account to that given by Jean Baudrillard in *Amérique*, published in 1986. In Baudrillard's account, 1980s North America is a zone of sexual permissiveness as a result of which everybody is in a state of indecision as regards their gender, and the levelling of sexual difference has become the norm, heralding a society of sexually autonomous, unisex individuals. In *Stone Butch Blues*, the same society is shown to be brutally intolerant of people whose appearance raises the question 'Is it a man or a woman?', and such people are shown to be living in constant fear for their lives. The presence of this danger is unexplored by Baudrillard and will serve as the primary context for considering vertical travel in *Stone Butch Blues* as exilic in origin.

In *Stone Butch Blues*, the narrator Jess Goldberg, a butch lesbian in pre-Stonewall Buffalo, New York, takes male hormones and has her breasts surgically removed in order to pass as a man. In this article I retain the author's terminology and refer to Goldberg as 'passing-male' as opposed to male or transsexual. This is to indicate that although she undergoes physical sex change, she does not consider herself to be a man. There is some ambivalence about her motives, to which I shall return, but the primary explanation she gives is as follows: she has been raped twice and subjected to so many severe beatings on account of her sexuality that she is physically and psychologically incapable of withstanding further attacks. She therefore tries to pass as a man to escape from the relentless gaybashing directed towards butch lesbians.

Stone Butch Blues opens with a retrospective letter, in which the transgendered narrator looks back on the events narrated in the main body of the novel from a distance of many years. In the very first paragraph of this letter, she defines her existence as exilic: 'Tonight I walked down streets looking for you in every woman's face, as I have each night of *this lonely exile*' (Feinberg 1993: 5). A few pages later, she is more specific. She says, 'Strange to be *exiled from your own sex* to borders that will never be home' (11). This is our first indication that the term exile refers to the condition of passing as a man. In this phrase, her 'own sex', that is, the one preceding hormone therapy, is posited as home and the subsequent one, the passing-male body, is posited as not-home. The autobiographical narrative goes some way to support the idea that the transition from the one to the other is consistent with notions of exile.

Firstly, Goldberg claims that for her, gender-realignment measures would ideally be used as a temporary subterfuge, not the actualisation of a desire to change sex. She distinguishes herself from female-to-male transsexuals, saying: 'I don't feel like a man trapped in a woman's body. I just feel trapped' (158–59). She asks whether it will be possible to 'go back to being a butch later, when it's safe to come out' (145). This model of escape is very much in line with Mary McCarthy's description of exilic status in 'A Guide to Exiles, Expatriates and Internal Emigrés': 'The exile waits for a change of government or the tyrant's death, which will allow him to come home. If he stops waiting and adapts to the new circumstances, then he is not an exile any more' (McCarthy 1994: 49).

Edward Saïd's essay *Reflections on Exile* includes rootlessness as a significant component of exilic experience: 'exiles are cut off from their roots, their land, their past' (Saïd 2001: 177). These are very much the terms in which experiences of passing as a man are described in *Stone Butch Blues*: 'I feel like a ghost...Like I've been buried alive. As far as the world's concerned, I was born the day I began to pass. I have no past, no loved ones, no memories, no me. No one really sees me or speaks to me or touches me' (213). Goldberg's first reaction to her condition as a passing-male is: ' I awoke feeling small and terrified. I couldn't find myself in my own life – there was no memory of me that I could grasp. There was no place outside of me where I belonged' (209). From these descriptions, Goldberg's life as a passing-male seems to be characterised by feelings of loneliness and a lack of belonging that are symptoms familiarly associated with exile.

If we are to accept Goldberg's experiences as constitutive of exile, then this is a departure from conceptions of exile as dependent on geographical displacement. In *Reflections on Exile*, one of the perspectives Saïd examines is that 'Exile is predicated on the existence of, love for, and bond with one's native place' (185). Within this alternative model being explored in *Stone Butch Blues*, 'native place' equals the human body. One of the ways in which I see *Stone Butch Blues* as potentially contributing to the redefinition of literatures of travel is in its integration of discourses of displacement into phenomena occurring initially on a physiological and psychological level within the human subject herself. That is, Goldberg's body exists as a site of travel, to the extent that her body is experienced as a vessel containing her mind and, as such, constitutes her mind's primary physical environment. Any change to that environment is liable to be experienced as a change of location.

As I am about to demonstrate, Goldberg hints at a new cartography which includes the bodies of the human beings that reside within geographical space. This expansion of understandings of what is properly constitutive of physical environment, and therefore amenable to non-metaphorical employment of discourses of displacement, is mirrored by recent innovations in the field of Cultural Geography. Contemporary cultural geographers are calling into question dualistic thinking that sees the body as necessarily separate from its surroundings and re-theorising relationships between internal and external space.

In a study entitled *Bodies: exploring fluid boundaries*, feminist geographer Robyn Longhurst makes a case for the full integration of the human body into considerations of what constitutes physical space (Longhurst 2001). She argues that the insides and outsides of bodies have a material reality and exist as actual physical locations. Similarly, bodily fluids and excreta exist as shifting boundaries and mobile features of the environment. Therefore, on account of its physical reality, any displacement inside or on the surface of the body and its fluids and solids should be considered as actual geographical displacement instead of being marginalised within geography or dismissed as theoretical.

These arguments, Longhurst says, are to be situated within the context of other attempts to give consideration to the body in geography, apparent in the work of certain geographers from the 1970s onwards. Longhurst acknowledges that 'over the last few years, geographers have begun to pay more attention to bodies' (1), but she criticises the theorised, abstract notion of the body that emerges from such work: 'The bodies articulated in geographers' texts have tended to be theoretical, fleshless bodies. A distinction has been drawn between discursive bodies and material bodies' (1–2). Longhurst claims that her work is innovative because, unlike earlier geographers, she gives attention to the biological reality of the body – 'the leaky, messy, awkward zones of the inside/outsides of bodies and their resulting spatial relationships [which] remain largely unexamined in geography' (2). She theorises geographers' neglect of such bodily realities as being deliberate and political in intention and effect, as it seems to her that such neglect perpetuates masculinist conceptions of knowledge which create antithetical associations between fluidity and irrationality, and solidity and rationality. Further, as we may infer from Longhurst's analysis, an appreciation of the body's spatiality would appear to be crucial to a feminist geography, to the extent that it would enable consideration of the boundary violence constituted by rape and sexual assault.

I now propose to explore some forms of body-centred departures featuring in Goldberg's narrative in the context of aggression towards lesbian subjects. Firstly, Goldberg's strategy for surviving rape is to be noted. While she is being raped, she uses increasingly sophisticated visualisation methods in order to imagine that she is somewhere else. On the first occasion, she successfully detaches her consciousness from the situation and focuses on her physical environment, then mentally reconfigures it as follows: 'I couldn't escape it, and so I pretended it wasn't happening. I looked at the sky, at how pale and placid it was. I imagined it was the ocean and the clouds were white-capped waves' (41). On a subsequent occasion, she focuses on a lightbulb and mentally transports herself to an elaborately-visualised desert. However, the pain and degradation which prompt these imagined journeys are simultaneously impeding freedom of visualisation: when the pain increases, she has to struggle for psychological mobility. In her words, 'I tried to return to the desert but I couldn't find that floating opening between the dimensions I'd passed through before. An explosion of pain in my body catapulted me back' (63).

In *Stone Butch Blues*, then, Goldberg's body is construed as a zone within which there can occur various forms of micro-displacement. It is, moreover, a zone with its own boundaries to be negotiated by other travelling bodies. Accordingly, *Stone Butch* sexuality, that is, the state of sexual unresponsiveness and guardedness supposedly resulting from long-term exposure to mental and physical harm, is presented as a walled landscape. Goldberg reflects on her sexuality in the following terms, to a prospective lover:

> There's a place inside of me where I've never been touched before. I'm afraid you'll touch me there. And I'm afraid you won't. My femme lovers knew me well, but they never *crossed those boundaries inside of me*. They tried to coax me *across the borders* into their arms (270).

The immobilised body is elsewhere also presented as trav-ellee of fluids: during the first rape, she is fused to the ground; she cannot run but she notes 'blood and slimy stuff *running* down her legs' (41), and describes how 'pain *travelled* up to [her] belly' (41). Male aggressors subject her to additional boundary violence across their own fluids and solids as she is urinated on and forced to eat excrement.

Earlier, I quoted Goldberg's comment, 'Strange to be exiled from your own sex to borders that will never be home' (11), which suggested that her diagnosis of her condition as exilic was strongly linked to the phenomenon of not feeling at 'home' in the passing-male body. Goldberg's usage of the word 'home' in the text as a whole both affirms the interpretation that the body is being experienced as location, and problema-tises any claim that the exile she designates is reducible to an enforced transition from one sex to another. The passing-male body is considered as 'borders that will never be home', but elsewhere Goldberg makes it explicit that in many ways the passing-male body *is* home. She describes the surgical removal of her breasts as a 'gift to [herself], a coming home to [her] body' (224). When testosterone has made her body lean and muscular, she claims to 'feel at home in [her] body' (171). There is also evidence that there had been an expectation that this would be the case. Before embarking on hormonal realignment processes, she has been idealising another passing-male whom she would like to regard, conceptually, as 'a home to come to when [she] wasn't safe' (96). This had been followed by a dream in which she was in a hormonally-altered body and 'felt happy in [this] body, comfortable among friends' (142).

There seems to be a degree of inconsistency and vagueness with regard to perceptions of home and their implications for Goldberg's conception of exile: I return to this later on. What does seem to be consistent is Goldberg's dualistic self-perception: she apparently considers herself in terms of consciousness dwelling inside a separate, alterable physical exterior. This dualistic self-perception is particularly conducive to intra-body travel – that is, types of travel in which the body itself is experienced as a changing location. Reflecting on her life as a passing-man, she describes this as a 'long road travelled', and says: 'I had never stopped looking at the world through my own eyes. I'd never stopped feeling like me on the inside. What if the real me could emerge, changed by the journey?' (222).

Although Goldberg paradoxically feels *more* at home in the altered body to which she has purportedly been exiled, her interpretation of her condition as being exilic is sustainable because of this novel's refusal to adhere to a unified notion of 'home'. One of the consequences of Goldberg's exile from a butch body into a passing-male body is that she is rejected by her femme lover, who refuses to be with somebody perceived to be male. This turn of events follows the pattern of traditional models of exile as based on banishment, as Goldberg is told to leave the house where they have been cohabiting, never to return. Without being designated as such, this appears in the light of a second exile contingent upon the first. At one point in the narrative, it is implied that this ex-lover represents home, as Goldberg states that 'the moments she pulled [her] head onto [her] lap and stroked [her] face were all [she] knew of refuge and acceptance' (223), and that there was nowhere else she could have gone 'for safety in an unsafe world' (223). However, she makes similar claims about other lesbian friends, gay bars and even her motorcycle, so attempts to privilege one or another seem provisional.

The body does not supersede external space as geography, it just adds another dimension: the transgendered subject's spatial body is simultaneously travelling in external space. It is of note that in *Stone Butch Blues*, external travel is presented as a strategy for living with the exilic condition. This disrupts the more familiar notion that external travel is a direct and regrettable consequence of exile. In her phase as passing-male,

Goldberg underlines the increased value she places on her Harley Davidson motorcycle. She says: 'I lived to cruise on that bike. It was my joy and my freedom' (209). Cruising can be seen as a motorised equivalent of flânerie, which serves in this case as an antidote to feelings of loneliness and isolation.

In the context of motorised recreational travel, transexuality is aligned with exile in terms of the motorcycle-owning transgendered subject's equivalent status as political alien. Goldberg loses the right to mobility because she cannot obtain identification reflecting her current gender as male. As a result, she cannot cross the border and she cannot even gain a valid motorcycle licence. The narrative focuses on a frustrated desire to travel, as the following example demonstrates:

> I still couldn't get across the border. I had no valid ID...I felt like a nonperson. I stared across the Niagara River, longing to open up my Harley on those roads I knew so well. A feeling of claustrophobia choked me. Even as my world was expanding, it was shrinking (175).

Goldberg continues to ride illegally within state boundaries rather than forgo the pleasure of motorised cruising. She refers to the motorcycle as a love object, saying, 'I love that bike. I mean, I actually love it' (52). Goldberg's attachment to the means of high speed motorised transport provides a valuable new context for the critical re-evaluation of the certain aspects of the work of French social theorist Paul Virilio. Arguably, Virilio's work is crucial to a critical appraisal of twentieth century travel literature as it addresses the social, political and personal implications of the technological advances that have brought about ever-increasing acceleration of displacements, communications and pace of living, including the advent of virtual reality and the Internet, as well as cars, motorcycles, aeroplanes and ballistic missiles.

Paul Virilio's work *Esthétique de la disparition* (1989) is of particular interest here as it features parallel discussions of the motorcycles and renegotiated sexual identities. Paul Virilio theorises the levelling of gender differences in the context of the rise of high-speed mechanised transport in the twentieth century. Virilio specifically links motorcycles, the disappearance of physical gender, and the demise of sexual relationships between men and women. He presents these as being related features of a society of ever-increasing speed. In Virilio's thought, Goldberg's transition from being attached to a woman to being attached to a motorcycle would be a logical progression in her given sociohistorical context. It is Virilio's contention that, in the context of love, people, specifically women, are being replaced by motors. 'L'engin remplace absolument la bien-aimée' (108). He illustrates this point with examples of people forming amorous attachments to cars and motorcycles. He claims that interrelationships are now modelled on a set 'trilogie' in which a *genderless* human subject accesses the world directly through motorised transport, bypassing any need for a human, sexual intermediary. This is said to have supplanted an earlier, biblical model consisting of Man being seduced by Woman and thereby attaining the World. 'La trilogie initiale est complètement modifiée et le rapport s'établit entre *un unisexe* (dissimulation définitive des identités physiologiques) et un vecteur technique, les contacts avec le corps de la bien-aimée [...] disparaissent' (104–05). Since men are removed from this equation in *Stone Butch Blues*, Goldberg's case problematises Virilio's masculinist conception in which the sexuality and travel practices of women are presented as always derivative and always based on an attempt to regain or replace the interest of men who now prefer motors to women.

Further, in *Stone Butch Blues* there seems to be a reversal of Virilio's premise that the motorbike represents the attraction of danger and accidents in a world that gives the illusion of being safe. Virilio describes how science has apparently created a society of sleepwalkers 'naturellement très à l'aise dans une situation de paix totale, de dissuasion nucléaire' (105). Goldberg, by contrast, expresses concerns about how to be safe in an unsafe world and, interestingly, the motorcycle is defined as a *place* of *safety*, as she says: 'Now this was the place I found my mobility and my safety – on this bike, under this helmet' (155). She finds comfort in high-speed cruising – similarly, on a train journey she observes: 'I began to feel the pleasure of the weightless state between here and there' (226).

On one level, certainly, Goldberg seems to be compensating for the lack of a fixed external 'home' by enacting Virilio's idea of dwelling in travel – 'installer dans le déplacement la fixité de la vie' (105). However, travel in physical space is also conceived of as a process of going home, where home is an unknown quantity yet to be encountered. She rationalises her will to travel as follows: 'The time had come to accept that my home might be waiting for me somewhere else. Or maybe I had to travel in order to find that home inside myself' (225).

Ultimately, 'home' appears to be a chaotic conception in this novel: vagueness and ambivalence with regard to where, what or who constitutes 'home' seems to be a defining feature of this text with significant implications for notions of travel and exile. Competing notions of home as body, home as acceptance, and home as mobility prove to be provisional.

Stone Butch Blues does, however, give us a clearer conception of what 'home' is not. That is, 'home' appears to be disassociated from cartography and chronology: it lacks topographical specificity, and is not the point of origin. Goldberg's place of birth and parental home are presented as a place of rejection, from which she migrates at the first opportunity towards the nearest gay community, in the hope of finding 'her people' for the first time.

Issues relating to differing sexual identities and the construction of notions of home and belonging are currently receiving attention in the field of Gay and Lesbian Studies, and affiliated branches of human geography. It is suggested that traditional conceptions of home are so firmly grounded in assumptions of heterosexual, patriarchal family structures that there is a need to renegotiate conceptions of home to reflect diversity of 'family' relationships and associated living arrangements. Of particular relevance to the problematisation of notions of home in *Stone Butch Blues* is an essay entitled 'Wherever I Lay My Girlfriend, That's My Home' by Lynda Johnston and Gill Valentine. This essay forms part of *Mapping Desire: geographies of sexualities*, a collection of studies addressing issues of sexual orientation and how it reconfigures human relationships to geographical space (Bell and Valentine 1995).

In 'Wherever I Lay My Girlfriend, That's My Home', Johnston and Valentine specifically explore the theoretical implications of lesbian sexualities for the concept of 'home'. It is argued that the parental home has 'no meaning as a source of identity or "roots"' because it is a site 'where heterosexual family relations act on and restrict the performance of a lesbian identity' (102–103). By contrast, it is argued, any locations permitting free performance of sexual identity may represent 'home' ipso facto. This creates the possibility of plural, interchangeable sites that may simultaneously be perceived as home.

The negative definition of home, applied to *Stone Butch Blues*, would suggest, by inference, a complementary negative definition of exile: the account of Goldberg's life from birth to running away from her parent's house at age sixteen is characterised by frequent, serious examples of exclusion and banishment, including care in foster homes, internment in a psychiatric hospital on account of her cross-dressing, exclusion from the school playground on account of being Jewish and then suspension from school. The narrator records these events but leaves them unanalysed and makes no attempt to interpret her conditions as exilic, apparently because throughout this stage of her life, it has been her primary, normative experience to feel like an outsider distanced by sexual orientation and gender dysphoria.

In conclusion, the premising of exile upon separation from a single, chronologically prior, location designated as home, or what Edward Saïd calls 'native place', is problematised by non-heteronormative conceptions of home, which may be plural and variable, and very often do not coincide with those communities to which one is affiliated by birth. Additionally, in the novel studied, gender dysphoria has been shown to reconfigure the subject's conception of physical space to include her body, which is posited as an alterable location. This creates the possibility of previously neglected, body-focused versions of both exile and other forms of displacement. These versions open up our understanding of travel as they constitute multilayered trajectories comprised of movement in both internal and external 'geographical' space.

References

Baudrillard, J. (1986) *Amérique*, Paris: Bernard Gasset. [Translated by Chris Turner (1988), as *America*, London: Verso.]

Bell, D. and G. Valentine (eds) (1995) *Mapping Desire: geographies of sexualities*, London: Routledge.

Feinberg, L. (1993) *Stone Butch Blues*, New York: Firebrand Books.

Longhurst, R. (2001) *Bodies: exploring fluid boundaries*, London and New York: Routledge.

Marin, M. (1987) *Le Saut de L'Ange*, Paris: Editions Fixot.

McCarthy, M. (1994) 'A Guide to Exiles, Expatriates and Internal Emigrés', in Robinson, M. (ed.), *Altogether Elsewhere: Writers on Exile*, New York: Harcourt Brace & Company.

Morris, J. (1974) *Conundrum: An Extraordinary Narrative of Transsexualism*, London: Henry Holt.

Saïd, E. W. (2001) *Reflections on Exile and Other Literary and Cultural Essays*, London: Granta Books.

Urbain J-D. (1998) *Secrets de voyage: Menteurs, imposteurs et autres voyageurs invisibles*, Paris: Essais Payot.

Virilio, P. (1989) *Esthétique de la disparition*, Paris: Editions Galilée. [Translated by Philip Beitchman (1991) as *The Aesthetics of Disappearance*, New York: Autonomedia.

CHAPTER 10

ANDY WARHOL AND THE STRATEGIC EXILE OF THE SELF

Chris Horrocks

There is nothing to say about Warhol, and Warhol has said just this in all his interviews and in his Journal, without rhetoric, without irony, without commentary – he alone being able to refract the insignificance of his images and his doings into the insignificance of his discourse. It is for this reason that whatever light one casts on the object Warhol, the Warhol effect, there is always something enigmatic about him which wrenches him out of the paradigm of art and the history of art (Baudrillard 1996: 75).

This essay will consider the subject of exile as a 'staged otherness' with reference to the performative and discursive actions of the artist Andy Warhol. I define 'exile' within the context of performative theory and theories of social action in order to describe how exile is socially performed. Warhol staged exile as a staging of the 'self-as-other' in relation to the context in which it appeared. Here, exile is viewed from a sociological perspective, as a situated, ongoing, inter-subjective process. Following a phenomenological model, this approach assumes that the social world is experientially interpreted by its members as meaningful and intelligible within social categories and constructs. I therefore treat exile as contingent and 'open to the situation' rather than as a fixed structure or referent. Exile cannot be defined in terms of the latter as such because it is an indeterminate and revisable process. It is therefore always incomplete.

I will employ the work of Erving Goffman and Harold Garfinkel in order to show how exile, loosely interpreted, can be approached within theories of social action. Both sociologists, while diverging on key methodological points, draw attention in different ways to the relation of the social agent to normative structures which provide the sense, meaningfulness or reasonableness of the social settings. In Goffman's work, the importance of the presentation of the social self within institutional settings is critical (see for example Goffman 1971, Garfinkel 1984). The use of role-play in general and the tactic of role-distancing in particular, are relevant to the social behaviour of Andy Warhol, because one feature of his version of exile is to divorce himself from social settings (while remaining 'inside' them) by distancing himself from his 'role'. In addition, the question of stigma, where the individual is cast outside the institutional frameworks defined by acceptable social behaviours, has relevance here.

In Garfinkel's case, this 'moral' injunction to socially normative behaviour is less an issue of institutional frames or norms than of the legibility of rules which social interaction constructs and typifies. I will consider Garfinkel's concept of 'breaching' in relation to the tactics that Warhol uses in specific social situations.

Garfinkel highlights the connection between the 'cognitive' content (here, common-sense social judgments) and the 'moral' force (the view of action as being the product of accountable moral choice). This is crucial, for it casts our study of Warhol's performance as a step-by-step affair according to socially standardised interactions where subjects are actively engaged in maintaining a 'world in common'. As we shall see, the moral dimension is important for the maintenance of the sense of social conduct. If it breaks down, and fails to be interpretable in accordance with the rules that are constantly fabricated and referred to in those actors' interactions (rather than with reference to an abstract set of rules imposed from outside), then the sense of the event is threatened.

Harold Garfinkel's 'breaching experiments', which destabilise the sense of situations in order to show how social structures are ordinarily maintained, have some significance for the moral or normative structures present in Warhol's social setting. I shall compare these experiments to Warhol's conduct in order to suggest that in effect Warhol operates as a reflexive agent in social interaction: Warhol himself consciously uses breaching experiments to draw attention to the sense-making and sense-breaking character of social interaction. My contention, with qualification, is that he uses this approach to reinforce the activity of role-distancing described above.

Finally, in order to make relevant the work of these sociologists to current debates on performativity I will briefly discuss the work of Judith Butler. This is important for our discussion of Warhol, for while performativity has many affiliations with theories of social action, it pushes to the foreground the role of discourse in regulating and materialising the gendered subject. It therefore makes plain the construction of the subject along a specific axis which, in labelling the subject (e.g. as 'queer'), positions that subject in a regulative regime. Sexuality and gender have recently become the dominant themes in constructions of Warhol's identity and a consideration of these typifications is essential to providing a contextual framework for considering Warhol's social world.

The labelling and naming of Warhol is a useful place to begin our analysis, for it is in the construction of Warhol through discourse that we can begin to consider his relation to a regulative, normative regime and to social action. We shall see that Warhol's incarnated otherness or his 'awayness' is just one aspect of a set of performative actions and utterances that not only register themselves at the margins of the rules dictating normative social behaviour, but also become the object of moral concern on account of their potential to breach those margins.

Constructing Warhol's Otherness

The overriding interpretation of Warhol has been his otherness or 'strangeness', his 'difference' within social settings, and his 'indifference' to them. In art theory, history, and criticism, and in autobiographical and biographical accounts of Warhol's identity, life, and world, the theme of otherness is expressed in ways that 'read off' Warhol's motives from his behaviour, such as his passivity in certain scenarios, or his reticence in interviews. There is plenty of anecdotal evidence to place Warhol as a peripheral character, both strangely present and absent. Indeed, Warhol himself puts this state of affairs forward as his existential being-in-the-world: 'Before I was shot, I always thought that I was more half-there than all-there – I always suspected that I was watching TV instead of living life' (Warhol 1977: 91).

Andy Warhol's presence, which is in some sense displaced and remote, is also connected to ambiguity. The ambiguous character of Warhol's being is consequently met with ambivalent interpretation: critics ascribe a wide, often contradictory range of meanings to Warhol's actions, statements, and art. For example, some readings cast his elusive, dispassionate social style as an absence that mirrors a psychological deficit. Kuspit, seizing on Warhol's statement that living life is like watching television because 'you don't feel anything' (Warhol: 91), analyses it as a regressively adolescent form in which mechanical acting out is accompanied by an inward turning off of feeling. Warhol's character and work are the epitome of 'aggressive depersonalisation'(Kuspit 1996: 72).

Warhol's persistence in displacing himself from his art, from direct confrontation with interviewers or associates, and from himself, was somehow consonant with a pathological condition. This is often invoked within anecdotal references to his close relationship to his mother or to his passive, 'sadistic' manipulation of his entourage. Emile de Antonio stated that: 'Andy was the Angel of Death's Apprentice as these people went through their shabby lives with drugs and weird sex and group sex and mass sex. So Andy looked and Andy as voyeur *par excellence* was the devil, because he got bored just looking' (Bockris 1998: 205). Here, for example, Warhol's tendency to remove himself from the events unfolding in his films, yet look on from beyond the frame signals a voyeuristic impulse for these critics.

The issue of Warhol's ambiguity – or more accurately the staging of his ambiguity – is closely associated with the theme of 'commitment' and 'alienation' which runs through critical readings. In this respect some writers interpret him less as an artist whose symptoms betrayed a psychological trauma than one whose alienation, and the traumatic repetition of his silkscreens, was performed reflexively as an affective deficit which amplified or mirrored traumatic social contradictions. Rainer Crone assessed his work and its alienation effects as operating according to Brechtian techniques, which registered its political intentions (Crone 1970; Crone and Wiegand 1972). Thomas Crow connected Warhol's early work, particularly the Disaster series of screenprints, to social upheaval (Crow 1987: 128–36), in order to suggest that Warhol's later work abandoned this aesthetic treatment of social issues in favour of a new role as portraitist to the rich, and accomplice of capital. This is echoed in Susan Sontag's reference to Warhol's lack of political compassion: 'I mean it wasn't possible for him to say, "That's terrible and I'm really against that and that shouldn't be." It's called capitalism. That [sic] saying it's OK. Don't tell me that Andy Warhol thought the Shah of Iran was a good guy. He couldn't. [...] What he did think was, "I don't have to worry about that question. That question is a boring question." And it was not a boring question if you had feelings' (Bockris 1998: 384).

Thus, in many approaches to Warhol's aesthetics, behaviour, and utterances, there persists an association between the Warhol-figure and his representation as damaged sexual subject whose persona and work were symptoms of social ills. His exploitation of key formal means (e.g., repetition) expressed the traumatic effect of social contradiction. The construction of Warhol as damaged subject assumes a moral injunction.

Andy Warhol, as subject of autobiographical and societal history, is remarkable for the breadth of interpretation along certain axes. For example, some critics from the left align Warhol with a revolutionary consciousness, while others draw the opposite conclusion that he is an accomplice of capital, albeit in alienated form. Others on the right, while connecting Warhol to ideology, forego the alienation model to register his postmodern sensibility with reference to his impersonality and his seamless connection to the socio-economic world around him. Robert Hughes is exemplary in this regard:

> To see Warhol entering a drawing room, pale eyes blinking in that pocked bun of a face, surrounded by his Praetorian Guard of chittering ingénues, is to realize that things do turn out rather well after all. [...] The alienation of the artist, of which one heard so much talk a few years ago, no longer exists for Warhol: his ideal society has crystallized round him and learned to love his entropy (Bockris 1998: 383).

Note also how Hughes' rhetoric ensures that the performative aspects of Warhol – here his appearance and manner – are introduced into the equation, functioning as incarnated signs of a narcissicistic indistinction between self and scene. These bodily appearances and actions are for Hughes no longer the expression of a modernist avant-garde disjunction between artist and social world which reserves to the artist an interiority and a subject position (albeit a perilous one). Instead, the artist as outsider, whose alienated consciousness enables him to reflect on and transform himself through artistic action, is replaced by what Donald Kuspit calls the 'adolescent' artist who is 'always "beside himself," acting "mechanically in a frenetic somnambulism"'(Kuspit 1996: 72).[1]

In various ways these interpretive strategies symptomatically read Warhol's body, actions and words in order to decode his 'motives' within a moral framework that places a negative emphasis on Warhol's political and sexual identity. The problem with this method is that it reduces Warhol to the acting out of an a priori libidinal economy or ideological structure. While these paradigms are germane to an understanding of Warhol's identity they fail to attend to *how* the acting out itself – the performative dimension – happens within the economy of everyday social interaction. A close description of the 'how' rather than the 'why' might permit us to bracket off the question of motive and morality and consider the situated character of the event.

I will draw on sociological method to achieve this, but in order to suggest that this approach has more than theoretical relevance to the description of Warhol's actions, I will place sociology in a historical context. Warhol and the theories of social action arise within a period in which social identity had become the object of enquiry. In many senses Warhol and postwar sociologists were interested in the same phenomenon: the rise of the individual as social performer within institutional contexts.

Historicising Social Action: Role-Play and Postwar America

The reason for using Goffmann's 'method' to study Warhol is not merely to cast more light over his 'enigma'.[2] There is also an important historical component, because Goffman's work emerged in the USA on the wave of a general interest, not to say concern, with the relationship of the individual to public and institutional life after the Second World War. His key text, *The Presentation of Self in Everyday Life*, identified a radical shift in the relation of self to society: social relations were organised more by the appearance than the content of things, including the self. Critics of the mass market and of corporate man saw that conformism, or what David Riesman in his book *Lonely Crowd* (1950) called 'other-directed' personalities, had replaced traditional American patterns of self-understanding and social interaction. The accumulation of symbols of prestige and lifestyle succeeded the inner world of self-improvement in personal life. Postwar managerial business practices in large-scale industry had been transformed by wartime organisational methods along open-ended, expansive, and non-structural lines. The issue of management was paramount and, as Caroline Jones (1996: 200) notes, culture responded in film, novels (e.g. *The Man in the Grey Flannel Suit*, Sloan Wilson, 1955), and non-fictional analyses (e.g. *The Organizational Man*, William H. Whyte, 1956) to the new figure of the corporate manager. This cultural production within academia, the business world, and the mass entertainment industry, 'delineated the concomitant pressures to conform to the manager's standards of sublimation and performance'.

In this scenario, the social critics began to use terms common within the new language of business, where 'impression management', 'teamwork', 'tacit agreement', 'familiarity' and 'performance' became integral components of the 'other-directed' corporate lexicon. Jones observes how artists in the postwar period similarly adopted managerial roles, running studios as a business. Warhol's 'Factory' is perhaps the most salient example of the elision of the traditional role of the artist as author or originator and the artwork as unique and handmade by the impersonal, 'team-worked' collective that produced mass-manufactured artwork.

The theorisation of the social subject as role-playing actor, whose identity was outwardly oriented and institutionally organised, became a dominant motif from the 1940s onwards. The moral and political implications of this social theory of action will now be discussed.

Role-Distancing: But Distancing From What?

'I do not dispute the direction in which things are going and I will go along with them, but at the same time I want you to know that you haven't fully contained me in the state of affairs' (Goffman, quoted in Lemert and Branaman 1997: 39–40).

The scenario Goffman presents above applies to the strategies that Warhol himself put into effect as situated tactics of his everyday world. With this principle in mind, I will now explore exile as a particular mode of dislocation or embodied and discursive displacement which Warhol established as a social and aesthetic tactic. Goffman called this ability of agents to signal their distinctions from roles ascribed to them 'role-distance'.

Saving of face, role distance, and role embrace, are methods and tactics that the individual uses to express attachment to or detachment from a role. Importantly this means that a subject can express disidentification with the role – the 'virtual' role – others have attributed to that subject. Yet, while the fundamental question is whether the self, as Goffman states, will 'go along' with the role, when speaking of role-distance we must also be aware of the normative, legitimating roles to which such strategic self-exiling refers. Goffman's study of stigmatisation and identity is relevant in this regard for it indicates that the role is capable of being 'credited or discredited' (Lemert and Branaman 1997: 24).

For Goffman, the subject's performance is always developed in relation to the possibility of stigmatisation. The self is a social product arising through what he calls 'validated performances', where social performers necessarily play active roles. Yet they must present images of themselves that can be socially supported, in the sense that the presentation of the self depends on validation rewarded or withheld in relation to social norms. Stigma is the cost of providing invalid performances for a social norm.

Recently, queer theory has related this earlier sociological work to the sexual politics of identity. As Sedgwick claims, for example, queer politics will carry the subtitle of Erving Goffman's book *Stigma: Notes on the Management of Spoiled Identity* (Doyle, Flatley and Muñoz 1996: 9). These theorists have argued that critics have interpreted Warhol's work in a stigmatising fashion, his art, career and subjectivity being read as somehow 'prostituted' or degraded. For the former, the moral consensus of the latter evinces their distrust of any deviation from a heterosexual norm or, more accurately, of the threat such deviations have to the integrity of that norm. Warhol's identity, conceived as sexually other, is defined as spoiled.

However, performative theory has provided more flexible accounts of the construction and maintenance of such spoiled identities. Whereas Goffman confines himself to studying the 'management' of a spoiled identity, performative theory emphasises not only its experimental, creative and performative force, but its *challenge to* the normative discourses that attempt to construct it as an abjected other. In terms of this norm, for example, Warhol's role-distancing has a specific inflection, because it is notable for the way its artificial or 'simulationist' properties can expose heterosexual imperatives as construction themselves. Queer writing on Warhol notes the parallel with Judith Butler's formulation of the logic of sexuality: 'Gay to straight is not as copy to original, but rather as copy is to copy' (Doyle, Flatley and Muñoz 1996: 10).

As Butler states, however, this logic should not be construed as reinstalling the social actor who makes up his or her identity from one moment to the next in an arbitrary, simulationist and postmodern fashion per se. Performativity is not an act of theatrical constructivism such that 'one woke in the morning, perused the closet or some more open space for the gender of choice, donned that gender for the day, and then restored the garment to its place at night' (Butler 1993: *x*). This fallacy reinscribes the voluntarist subject who decides on its gender. Instead, we should recognise how the subject is already decided by gender, and how the body of the subject is materialised (i.e. is not simply a discursive or linguistic construction) as 'the effect of a dynamic of power, such that the matter of bodies will be indissociable from the regulatory norms [such as the heterosexual imperative] that govern their materialisation and the signification of those material effects' (Butler 1993: 2).

However, the fact that the subject is indissociable from regulatory norms does not necessary mean that the regulatory norm has it all its own way when contriving to stigmatise non-normative sexualities. The strategic, situated expression of the stigmatised subject in his or her relation to the regulative norm can be better understood if we acknowledge that performative tactics involve a partial, often subversive investment in the significatory practices of, for example, the heterosexual regime. They can be illuminated with reference to a concept central to performative theory after Goffman: 'disidentification'. Recently, the term has been used by Muñoz in his essay 'Famous and Dandy', which discusses the use of disidentificatory practices by Warhol and in Jean-Michel Basquiat's painting (Doyle, Flatley and Muñoz 1996: 144–179).

The significance of disidentification lies in the ability of a subject such as Warhol not only to identify with or against the regulatory norm (e.g. heterosexuality), but also to exploit it or recycle it to other ends. Disidentification is a strategy that works both on and against dominant ideology. It signals neither a joining in nor a departure from the dominant ideology. Although heterosexuality can ensure its hegemony by permitting its denaturalisation (e.g. in drag performance), it is also the case that the occupation of this denaturalisation by subjects can bring about a site of resistance. For example, the word 'queer' can be reaffirmed less as a citation that constrains than as political possibility.

In many ways Goffman's concept of role-distance (going along with things while signifying that one is not constrained by them) approximates disidentification (working on and against things). The difference, though, lies in the emphasis that the latter places on recycling or reusing the significations of the dominant norm rather than simply signalling a territory of identity that is preserved in the face of the norm. Disidentification is much more a process geared to fabricating identities from the given texture of signifying practices than to preserving identities in spite of them.

For the purposes of analysing Warhol's performative tactics both of these tools are important. Role-distance is relevant because it enables us to frame his social action as performatively geared towards constructing a space of relative independence within social settings. Disidentification is critical because it shows us that role-distantiation can be effected by using the normative fabric of social interaction and destabilising it at the same time. A description of Warhol's performative tactics might show us how the two approaches operate in tandem within the life-world of a single social subject.

Warhol's Tactics

'The image of him that is generated for him by the routine entailed in this mere participation – his virtual self in the context – is an image from which he apparently withdraws by *actively* manipulating the situation' (Goffman, quoted in Lemert and Branaman 1997: 37).

What techniques did Warhol use, unconsciously or consciously, to distance himself from himself, and from the virtual roles allotted to him by others? How did they use or challenge dominant models of conduct? These can be divided into three heuristic categories: physical (embodied or incarnated); positional (situational or environmental); and discursive (linguistic or conversational). I will mention the first two only in passing, as the issue of language is the most important for the purposes of this essay, and for the reason that Warhol's use of language is rarely discussed.

The first involves gesture, pose, and expression. Warhol's hexis, or bodily disposition, is used to divorce his self from the immediate social situation.[3] His posturing is most pronounced when conducted for aesthetic reasons, including his pose for photographs, or his celebrated appearance as a living Warhol sculpture in a gallery window. In other examples, his folded arms, use of sunglasses to break eye-contact, or placement of hand to cover his mouth construct barriers against the scene around him.

In terms of positionality, Warhol often physically situated himself 'off to one side'; either perched on the edge of a sofa, or standing at the periphery of the gallery or studio. He would spend hours propped up against the wall talking on the Factory phone, which was placed next to the exit. His directorial role in his films is a significant example of Warhol's detachment from events taking place in front of the camera (and, indeed, often behind it).

Another form of role-play as role-distance is Warhol's use of conversation, when he removes himself discursively from the situation. This tactic has several components. The first is one of reticence. This is simply Warhol acting dumb or mute in the face of an interviewer or a group conversation. The second is incomprehension, where he affects not to understand the question or the 'rules' of interaction and 'blanks' the interlocuter and thus the situation. The third is vagueness or diversion, where he answers obliquely or strays from the point. The final, most celebrated one is generalisation, where he answers a specific question with an expansive statement (when asked what he thought of photography, for example, he replies that 'gee, all photos are great').

The discursive aspect of Warhol's disidentification bears a striking resemblance to Garfinkel's ethnomethodology of everyday interaction. Garfinkel's contribution to the theory of social action showed how social agents interacted on the shared assumption that they were actively maintaining a world in common according to constitutive rules. This interaction is sustained only in the absence of counter-evidence. In other words, agents proceed on the assumption that they understand the situation and that the other person understands them. However, when an action (say, a sentence within a conversation) fails to make sense in the context of the conversation, the agent attempts to reinterpret the rules along new lines (e.g., 'he couldn't have heard me properly'). Garfinkel turned these 'breaches' into methodological tools.

His 'breaching experiments' reversed the sociological method
of discussing the stability of social actions and looking for
variables that contributed to it. He stated:

> An alternative procedure would appear to be more economical:
> to start with a system with stable features and ask what can be
> done to make for trouble. The operations that one would have
> to perform in order to produce and sustain anomic features of
> perceived environments and disorganized interaction should
> tell us something about how social structures are ordinarily and
> routinely being maintained (Heritage 1984: 78).

For example, in one famous experiment he asked his students
to pretend to be therapists and answer questions from
unwitting volunteers, who received arbitrary 'yes' or 'no'
responses. The volunteers rationalised these random responses
in order to render them meaningful. They did so in order to
normalise the discrepancies that arose. In other experiments
the interactional breakdown was more catastrophic. Students
were told to engage in conversation with friends but insist that
the latter clarify the sense of their commonplace remarks:

> The victim waved his hand cheerily.
> Subject: How are you?
> Experimenter: How am I in regard to what? My health, my
> finance, my school work, my peace of mind, my ...
> Subject: (Red in the face and suddenly out of control.) Look!
> I was just trying to be polite. Frankly, I don't give a damn how
> you are (Heritage 1984: 80).

The breach demonstrates that in all cases much of what is
talked about is not mentioned, although each person expects
that the adequate sense of the matter being talked about is
settled.

One filmed interview dating from the mid-1960s exemplifies Warhol's tactics of displacement. It is typical because it
shows how, in disidentificatory, role-distancing style he
detaches himself from the sense of the event by drawing on
and recycling its content. In this instance, Warhol is being
interviewed about his work. The interviewer asks a question
(about the content of an exhibition) which requires a 'yes' or
'no' response. Warhol replies 'yes'. To the next question
Warhol replies 'no'. The interview, and Warhol's answers, still
makes sense at this point. However, after several more
responses it becomes obvious that Warhol is simply answering
'yes' or 'no' alternately.[4]

The interviewer seems oblivious to Warhol's constructivist approach to the interview situation, perhaps for good reason. In dialectical fashion, Warhol's tactic of pre-planned alternate negative and affirmative responses is intelligible within the logic of the questions being asked, and the interview format. He could have replied 'yes' or 'no' and the conversation would still have made sense. However, Warhol still manages to manufacture the situation in order to show the normative rules of the discursive code in which he was placed, and to dissociate his self from it 'while going along with it' and while actively 'using it'. Other strategies follow this logic, including his mechanical responses in interview situations, and his vagueness, posing passivity, indirectness and other forms of diversion (e.g. getting his friend to reply to questions which have been directed at Warhol).

Warhol's breaching and role-distance therefore display a dimension absent in most accounts of performativity: humour. His displacements of self are often mobilised with a comic intention. As Warhol says, 'usually being the right thing in the wrong space and the wrong thing in the right space is worth it, because something funny always happens' (Warhol 1977: 158). Whatever the comic content or motives of such tactics, Warhol performs using techniques of displacement (including reflectivity and mimicry) in order to disrupt the smooth workings of discourse. His performance is the height of artifice, but it is not confined to his own artificiality. The act is used to register the artifice of the social norm (much as his screenprints exposed the constructed character of stardom or fame). His tactic is one that illuminates neither the content of a social situation, nor his own content or agency, but exposes the form or the framing devices in which his tactics operate.

However, the frame, or rule-oriented context within which social interaction takes place has a particular complexion in Warhol's world. This is because it is rarely the case that Warhol is acting in contexts over which he has little control (unlike, for example, Goffman's example of the mental patient within an institutional setting). Warhol's frame(s) implies a specific dimension in terms of role-distance and disidentification because these tactics are performed in circumstances which are in a sense organised by him in advance. In other words, Warhol's otherness was bound up with his facility to make the social context his own. He became the dominant member of a space, which included the Factory, the gallery, the party and the film set. This 'territoriality', as Goffman calls it, of Warhol's habitus – particularly the arrangement of the Factory – constituted a complex stage that enabled Warhol to extend his role-play into his surroundings and incorporate his surroundings into his role-play. In a sense, he occupied the frame that Goffman says most people work within, for or against, and there were many frames through which Warhol passed, including his directorial role at the Factory, his role within an interview setting and his role at parties.

With the Factory, Warhol produced what Goffman would call a 'stage', which operated according to rules that could be generated ad hoc and without direct accountability to those of the 'total institutions'. Indeed, the rules of interaction were produced out of a combination of the overlapping frames of business, subculture and art. Warhol's territoriality was therefore of a uniquely 'extended' kind, and being so, it provided more scope for his role-distancing actions.

Warhol's tactics thus enable him to construe himself in a kind of voluntary exile, though one which is never in a space apart from the scene in which they are enacted. This is for two reasons. First, the role-distancing requires disidentification, and the latter is by definition a process which recyles significations that are available to the social agent (here, Warhol) in the scene. It is through disidentification that Warhol can be both 'here' and 'away'. Furthermore, in the performance of this distancing Warhol exposes the 'rules of the game' by his use of breaching behaviour. Secondly, Warhol is never out of the frame because in many cases he was able to manipulate the 'scenery' in which his action took place.

Conclusion

These displacements and forms of performed alienation in social settings are central to Warhol's construction and deconstruction of his self and his scene. Indeed, following Warhol's observation in *The Philosophy of Andy Warhol*, it can be claimed that his modus operandi (to quote him on his films) 'showed you how some people act and react with other people. They were like actual sociological "For instances"' (Warhol 1977: 48). He drew attention through his actions to the framing and frame-breaking processes inherent in social and aesthetic practices.

Warhol's use of displacement, disidentification and role-distancing can be viewed as a set of strategies deployed tactically either reflexively or through habit memory to destabilise or reconfigure norms or rules in an improvisatory manner within a series of frames or settings which are themselves staged and framed by and through Warhol. By displacing himself through pose and discourse, Warhol draws attention to the constructive and arguably normative discourse that seeks to pin him down and bring him to account. The evasive quality of his performance is not simply a mask behind which a 'real Warhol' can be discerned, but a means by which people ascribe his motives to an agency behind his 'front'. Some critics construed these techniques of displacement immanent to this front as being reflective of a damaged subjectivity or a 'fractured' self.

However, one can also suggest that these techniques are organised to dismantle or destabilise regulatory imperatives that Andy Warhol and his peers worked against and within. As Butler notes, normative discourse is always abject and reiterates the other, such as the queer subject. This discourse draws attention to the instabilities that exist within dominant ideology. Butler's view is valid, as far as it goes (it tends to reduce the performative to the question of gender). But sociology, in some respects, reveals more about how normativity itself becomes contested by its other, and strategically colonised by it, according to situated yet contingent and mobile tactics that may arise within a specific individual's performance of a singular type of 'exile'.

Notes

1. Kuspit is quoting from José Ortega y Gasset, 'The Self and Other' (1939), in *The Dehumanization of Art and Other Writings on Art, Culture and Literature*, Garden City, New York: Doubleday, 1950: 164.
2. As Charles Lemert says, 'One of the most unimaginative complaints against him [Goffman] is that he had no replicable method ... there are in Goffman no facts as we normally construe them. At best, there are definitions, but these are always quirky like universal human nature itself. Goffman's definitions are really moves against the grain of readerly expectations' (Lemert and Branaman 1997: x).
3. I borrow this term from Pierre Bourdieu. 'Bodily hexis is political mythology realized, *em-bodied*, turned into a permanent disposition, a durable manner of standing, speaking and thereby of *feeling* and *thinking* ...' (Bourdieu 1977) However, unlike Bourdieu's concept, which relegates hexis to an unconscious process, I wish to emphasise its reflexive, conscious function.

4. See the television documentary, *This is Modern Art*, Part 1, Channel 4, UK (2001).

References

Baudrillard, J. (1996) *The Perfect Crime*, London and New York: Verso.

Butler, J. (1993) *Bodies that Matter: On The Discursive Limits of 'Sex'*, London and New York: Routledge.

Bockris, V. (1998) *The Life and Death of Andy Warhol*, London: Fourth Estate Limited.

Bourdieu, P. (1977) *Outline of a Theory of Practice*, Cambridge: Cambridge University Press.

Crone, R. (1970) *Andy Warhol*, New York: Praeger.

Crone, R. and W. Wiegand (1972) *Die revolutionäre Ästhetik Andy Warhols*, Darmstadt: Melzer Verlag.

Crow, T. (1987) 'Saturday Disasters: Trace and Reference in Early Warhol', *Art in America* (75)5 (May 1987), 128–36.

Doyle, J., J. Flatley, and J. E. Muñoz (eds) (1996) *Pop Out: Queer Warhol*, Durham and London: Duke University Press.

Garfinkel, H. (1984) *Studies in Ethnomethodology*, London: Polity.

Goffman, E. (1971) *The Presentation of the Self in Everyday Life*, Harmondsworth: Penguin.

Heritage, J. (1984) *Garfinkel and Ethnomethodology*, Cambridge: Polity.

Jones, C. A. (1996) *Machine in the Studio: Constructing the Postwar American Artist*, Chicago and London: University of Chicago Press.

Kuspit, D. (1996) *Idiosyncratic Identities: Artists at the End of the Avant-Garde*, Cambridge: Cambridge University Press.

Lemert, C. and A. Branaman (eds) (1997) *The Goffman Reader*, Massachusetts and Oxford: Blackwell.

Riesman, D. (1950) *Lonely Crowd: A Study of the Changing American Character*, New Haven, Connecticut: Yale University Press.

Warhol, A. (1977) *The Philosophy of Andy Warhol (From A to B and Back Again)*, San Diego, New York and London: Harvest.

CHAPTER 11

EXILES OF NORMALITY: PHOTOGRAPHY AND THE REPRESENTATION OF DISEASED BODIES

Richard Sawdon Smith

The human body has been represented by photography for more than a century and a half and it is through photography, more than any other medium, that we have shaped our notions of the modern body.[1] Issues of sexuality, gender and self-identity are bound up within photographic representations, as are issues of ideology, politics and power. Control over the production and dissemination of images has been at the heart of debates for many artists and writers since the late 1960s. In particular much has been done to question the validity of uses of photography in nineteenth century institutions as the social and cultural history of photography has been continuously rewritten. Influenced by Michel Foucault's historical analysis many writers have explored the relationship between photography and power, concerned with representation as a fundamental tool in control of the criminal, the sexual deviant and the diseased body.[2] These invisible histories exiled to the archive highlight the splitting of science from the popular art-historical discourse of photography. We are much more likely to discuss photography of the female body in terms of an 'artistic' nude than consider the implications of a doctor's diagnostic image of a breast cancer patient. This is due in part to the fact that we are unlikely to see these images,

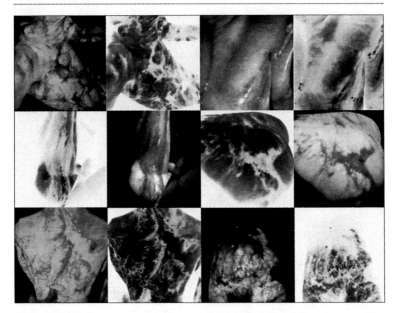

Figure 11.1 Symptom (*sinthome*), 1997 © Richard Sawdon Smith.

as they are controlled in the archive for those who are deemed to have the knowledge to access them. It is no coincidence that during the last twenty years this period of questioning photography and power has coincided with the discovery and naming of AIDS, since when writing on the body has become more mainstream.

As a practising photographer, confronted with issues of appropriateness of exhibiting and publishing what some describe as uncomfortable and disturbing images, I have been forced to question the construction of 'normality' within our society, and how deviation from the norm can result in a silencing of individuals and groups who do not fit in with, and are therefore exiled from, the socially constructed ideal of the beautiful, healthy, good body. The basis for this chapter lies in a series of photographs produced in 1996/1997 called 'Symptom (*sinthome*)',[3] which tried to deal with the emotional and psychological impact that a HIV positive diagnosis had on the body and the mind. The work was dealing with the absence of any physical symptoms of illness. The apparently healthy body marginalised once the disease was named: HIV would bring to the 'minds eye', rather than the outward physical appearance, a catastrophe of representations created by living in a culture that is so alienated from the body. In the case of HIV and AIDS these images can become tainted by the rhetoric of homophobia, racism and the otherness of the diseased body. By this I mean we recognise the healthy body and therefore by extension ourselves by what we are not: ugly, evil, corrupting. The realisation of a loss or lack of control over the body, so often articulated by people when diagnosed with a serious illness, is projected away from the body in an attempt to capture and tame it. The 'Symptom' series shows images of the interior of a diseased body projected on to the surface of another. Positive and negative images looking towards the visceral depths of the body trying to make visible the invisible. The work was also influenced by the theorist Hal Foster's comments on contemporary art, theoretical concerns and fascination with trauma and the abject. In his paper 'Obscene, Abject, Traumatic' published in 1996, informed by Julia Kristeva's influential book *Powers of Horror* about abjection, he states that because of the despair about the persistent AIDS crisis, increased disease and death in the world, 'a special truth seems to reside in traumatic or abject states, in diseased or damaged bodies. To be sure, the violated body is often the evidential basis of important witnessing of truth, of necessary testimonies against power' (Foster 1996: 122–23). Foster indicates a crucial ambiguity in Kristeva's theory between the subject being able *to abject* and the condition *to be abject*. While abjection is a necessary condition of survival, 'the abject is what I must get rid of in order to be I at all' (Foster 1996: 114), to be abject would imply the subject already an exile of society. Part of the language concerning AIDS and the body in the 1980s and early 1990s was to do with abjection because of the suffocating presence of death. In the light of combination therapy the language is of process and change. At the time of producing the 'Symptom' series I was asked by a friend, Simon Kennett, to photograph him, or more precisely to document his changing body. Although protease inhibitors, the drugs used in combination therapy, had been introduced at this time, Simon would not risk the side effects while his health was returning. Simon did have full blown AIDS and the images of him spoke in a different dialect to those dealing with HIV. In fact they are almost the opposite, they are punctuated with the visible signs of illness, as if everything was written on the surface of the body. Daniel Canogar writing in the exhibition catalogue about the work of Anthony Aziz and Sammy Cucher, who digitally manipulate the contours of the skin, sealing various orifices of the models in their photographs, points out that the skin is like an 'elastic surface that reveals even as it conceals: as if gazing through a veil', and in terms of a classification of the AIDS body 'society reads these epidermic lesions as evidence of deviant sexual practices' (Canogar 1999: 262).

Absent Bodies/Present Lives

Through medical discourse a definition of the 'Other' has been formed around what the healthy are not – illness as the antithesis or absence of health. The healthy body is the 'norm', and 'abnormal' bodies are not considered the subject for photography unless for medical and scientific reasons. This results in the construction of an institutional gaze deciding what the problem is and how to deal with it: the photograph silencing the subject. However a definition of 'normal' is always considered by what it is perceived not to be, the 'abnormal'. The self then becomes constructed by the 'Other', in this example the diseased or damaged body, but the body that is absent to us, that is never under investigation, is the healthy body.

Awareness of our bodies appears to be, at the very best, temporal. We function in society by being unaware of our own body. Drew Leder has argued, in his book *The Absent Body* (1990), that this absence is necessary for functioning. It would be impossible to live while considering every movement and positioning of our body especially if we were to try and comprehend the internal at the same time. Leder sums up the body's tendency to disappear from awareness and action with the terms 'ecstatic' where by the body projects outside of itself into the world, and 'recessive', when the body falls back from its own conscious perception and control. In addition he also points out that the body simply 'moves off to the side' when surface parts of it are not in action (Leder 1990: 69). However the most interesting analysis is when Leder considers what he calls the 'dys-appearing body'. The conspiracy of silence we adopt about our own body is broken when it becomes diseased or damaged, but even then we may not relate to this broken body as ours. He writes: 'Insofar as the body seizes our awareness particularly at times of disturbance, it can come to appear "Other" and opposed to the self' (Leder 1990: 70). This aspect has been crucial for many people confronted with their own illness. If we understand the body to be absent while healthy, forced into consciousness the effects can be traumatic beyond the conditions of ill-health. Not only would this have to take into account notions of the repressed but also the effects of social and cultural histories on the body. Jo Spence was one artist, or cultural sniper as she preferred to be called, who tried to express in her work these conflicting feelings by creating what she termed a 'subjective language'. Her work, particularly around cancer, not only brought into question the lack of control she felt as a patient within the medical institution but the very lack of a body. Even after years of producing work that questioned the representations of women in society Spence felt she had only 'superficially' been aware of her own body while now it could be said to become the 'evidential basis of important witnessing of truth' (Foster 1996: 123).

Drawing on Drew Leder's account of the 'absent body', it is suggested that, even in the phenomenological tradition of Merleau-Ponty, 'which stresses the unity of matter and mind expressed through the being-in-the-world of bodies, the healthy body, far from being consistently present to us, is scarcely experienced at all' (Shildrick 1996: 3). It is when the body becomes diseased or damaged that it seizes our attention, and the attention of others, most strongly. The body forces itself into our consciousness at times of dysfunction and that comfortable absence is lost. It dys-appears; i.e. appears in a dysfunctional state. The body is now perceived but experienced as other, creating a dys-juncture with 'normal' bodily state of dis-appearance.

Although this goes some way to understanding the shock of confrontation with the body when diseased or damaged Leder's is a regional ontology of the body, discussing how alienation of the body from the self occurs. As Leder puts it, 'the body is no longer alien-as-forgotten, but precisely as re-membered, a sharp searing presence threatening the self' (Leder 1990: 91). Leder's phenomenological account of the body has drawn a response from a number of sociologists (Schildrick 1996: 3, Williams 1998: 77, Corker 1999: 77, Overboe 1999: 27) who have questioned the extent to which his theories can be implemented. In summary it can be said that, although all bodies have the potential of corporeal irruption into consciousness, the being of any/body that is 'Other' heightens the threat and therefore it is not simply the possibility of the broken body that disrupts the boundaries of the transcendent subject. While Leder's analysis describes a certain universal structuring of bodily experience it does not recognise that apprehension of the body, or lack thereof, is shaped in a thousand ways by one's material, social and cultural environment, as well as by the body's capacity for pleasure. To suggest that our body is absent from daily consciousness does not fully recognise what it is to be a woman, or black, or old, or disabled, or gay in the society we live in.

Exiles of Normality

It was the response in the media to a particular image of Simon that highlighted the problematic discourses surrounding photographic representations of the diseased or damaged body still existing in the twenty-first century. This discussion took place in the public arena, in newspapers, photographic magazines, books, on the radio and television, and therefore it seems appropriate to use this photograph here as a case study.[4] The black and white image is a full-frontal naked portrait of Simon with his body facing the camera/spectator. In this image, however, he does not confront the viewer with his own gaze but looks down, as if reflecting on his now 'deformed' changing body. Standing in the centre of the picture supported by a walking stick and on a black archival box, his body stands out against the black backdrop of the studio. The body is obviously swollen, particularly the legs, feet and genitals – the effects of water retention due to his condition, and a problem, therefore, of being unable to abject.

This image was selected as the winning portrait in the 1997 John Kobal Award, a prestigious competition attracting international entries, and exhibited at the National Portrait Gallery in London. However the media sponsor of the award, *The Times* Saturday newspaper, which normally publishes the winner, refused to print the image, stating that it was 'too disturbing'.[5] The photograph then became a news item in terms of its suitability for publication. An entire letters page of *Amateur Photographer (AP)* magazine[6] was devoted to responses to the image, all critical, one accusing it of pandering to the taste of those who would have enjoyed a 'freak show'. It was seen as inappropriate subject matter for publication – fellow photographers should not wish to emulate this type of image. Apart from some other generally homophobic and anti-AIDS comments the same letters page carried a response from a doctor who referred to the photograph as a 'medical illustration' which breeches 'normal' tasteful and artistic boundaries. So we have to ask; if Simon is not an 'appropriate' photographic

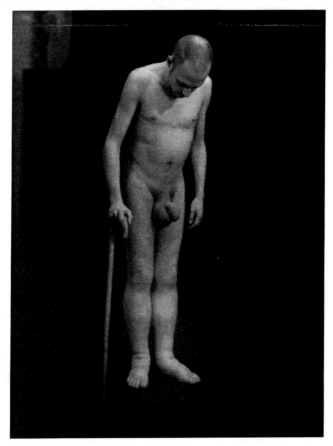

Figure 11.2 Simon '97, 1997 © Richard Sawdon Smith.

subject, what is he? Does this mean that Simon himself is outside of 'normal' boundaries and if so; who sets the boundaries?
He is exiled by a collective fantasy of what our society should
and should not include, historically informed by a medical
and scientific fallacy of the norm. At the height of paranoia
about the potential of an AIDS epidemic in the West there
were calls for not just people with AIDS but all gay men to be
quarantined – put on an island away from and to protect the
rest of society. This would need to involve a system of identifying, making visible, those people it then intended to vanish.
The same process can be seen as one way in which the medical
image of the 'abnormal' body is quarantined to the safety of
the archive in an act of 'representational liquidation'
(McGrath 1995: 99).

A letter from Roy, another reader of *AP*, this time reflecting on a photograph of himself after an accident, sees no merit in such an image either. On the surface this indicates a belief that the photograph as document has no value outside of its intended meaning, but it also belies a disassociation of the diseased or damaged body as different. A body now apprehended as alien from the self – not of me, but of my diseased or damaged body – it has now dys-appeared. On the surface there are some fundamental differences between the image of Roy and that of Simon. While Simon had personally requested the representation of his body, Roy remembers 'posing' for the doctors after they had 'reassembled' him. The choice of words reveal that in 'posing' this was not considered a 'normal' or 'natural' photograph, destined, perhaps, for the family album (the most controlled and constructed archive we know), but for the doctors so that they could admire their handiwork. An image of recovery, a body returning to the productive world, while Simon's image, although about recovery for himself, will never enter the same world.

Beyond the medical surgery, a place where a doctor may come across similar conditions in the flesh, so to speak, the representation of Simon is questioned. Writing in to *AP*, the Doctor, a prefix we associate with power and knowledge, assumes dual roles, one from a position of authority and one as an amateur photographer, creating mixed messages as to why such an image is inappropriate. Would the doctor inform Simon if he was one of his patients that he could not be represented outside of the surgery, as if he did not exist, and would this be on medical or artistic grounds? It was suggested, by another man writing to *AP*, that a female portrait would be a more appropriate subject matter, because it would be 'artistic and a genuine reflection of the photographers craft'. The same person also proposed and answered his own question, 'would a similar photo of a cancer victim have been considered? I think not...'. It is clear from these quotations that the photographer is expected to be male and the object of his gaze female, as in the best traditions of art history, and that representations should be of suitably pre-described aesthetic qualities to be considered art. While the views expressed in *AP* have little to do with the cutting edge of art or photographic representation, it needs to be taken seriously as a sign of the depth of prevalent attitudes in society to both the body and its image. The image of Simon is placed outside the dominant art-historical discourse about photography, partly because it is a parody, and read through the medical and the condition it illustrates. Although, as the writer and critic Simon Watney (1987: 1) explains, the same photograph of the same body can have different readings depending on whether it is interpreted by a doctor, a sociologist or an anthropologist, or, for that matter, a lay person. The image of Simon appears to become problematic because it does not conform to the preconceptions of what makes a good photograph, as it is the unhealthy male depicted nude tearing away at the construction of male power. The fact that Simon's genitals are swollen and therefore unproductive increases the sense of vulnerability and powerlessness, a sort of reversed castration complex.

Simon spoke of the fact that he did not see himself as different from anybody else. The physical presence of his body, the exterior social interacting part of him, may look different to how it used to be but he was still the same person underneath. He came to terms very quickly with what we might describe as a social body and the body self, perceiving this difference as 'the world's' problem and not his. It is this attitude and the immediacy of his body that makes it a difficult image as it dismantles the distance demanded by parody. As a critique aimed at the historical institutional practices of classification and categorisation of people because they appeared to be outside of the 'norm', it is surprising how strongly the influence of these practices is still felt today, in some cases manifesting itself as an extremely hostile reaction. The image of the body in crisis interrupts the absent indifferent body of the spectator as images encountered in art have traditionally required a recessive body from its audience. Clearly in this case part of the reaction was because the cause of Simon's disfigurement was made known to be AIDS-related and by implication his sexuality came into question. The circle is then closed in the minds of some people. Unlike the cancer 'victim', although this could be challenged, the sexual deviant has proved the pathology of its diseased and corrupting body.

Enfreakment

It is interesting that the apparently disparate comments from amateur photographers mentioned earlier created an association of the medical image with that of the 'freak show'. The implication being that, those who are unhealthy should be classified as a 'body apart' from a 'collective body'. People with disabled or disfigured bodies, once a spectacle to gaze upon, are now not even to be represented in society. While we tend to distance ourselves today from these earlier practices, our selective history of photography denies, as Roberta McGrath has observed in her historical study of nineteenth-century medical pictures, that photography grew out of and as part of the anatomical museums, cabinets of curiosities, displays of magic, dioramas and phantasmagoria. To the general public photography was the latest in a succession of amazing spectacles of magic (McGrath 1995: 104).

As we have split art from science so we have split the diseased body from the healthy body. The development of modern medicine coincides with the rise of photography and the importance of visual representations in aid of diagnosis. Therefore the distance from and rationalisation of the body as the object of investigation within the medical model equates it as the mindless, emotionless body of Cartesian dualism. This model has implications outside of medicine, as Sander Gilman has convincingly put it in a number of books examining images as spaces in which history is made and enacted. In *Health and Illness: Images of Difference* (1995) Gilman clearly demonstrates the link between the medical idea of the healthy body and the 'normal', (re)productive body of society. The good citizen is the one who will not pose a threat to the rest of society. A consequence of these practices led to the belief in society that the unhealthy must be 'abnormal' and therefore bad. This threat of infection was not limited to just physical illness but included the insane, the criminal, the sexual pervert, generally any of society's 'undesirables'. The progression of these ideas led to the establishment of the pseudo-science of eugenics. This science proposed that facial characteristics could reveal inherent truths about the individual and relied on photography to provide evidence for these beliefs: beliefs that incorporated the notion of a pure race.[7]

While we can understand the idea of illness as a contamination, a pollutant that could infect the healthy, we must also consider that the ill are perceived as something that should not be there, something that is in the wrong place. This is a hypothesis based on the work of Mary Douglas, in *Purity and Danger* (1995), who explores the qualities of dirt, which we could substitute for notions of illness. What makes dirt dirty is not its substantial form but because it should not be there, it is not in its proper place. Dirt is a by-product of a systematic ordering and classification of matter in so far as ordering involves rejecting inappropriate elements, the rejected elements of ordered systems. In this instance the exiled elements are the diseased and damaged bodies, metaphors of disorder, dys-function, excess, corruption and unnaturalness. However, a number of artists have produced work that directly challenges this ordered system. One of the most prominent being Spence, who has 'tried to reconnect parts of ourselves that have become subjected to the process of splitting and hierarchisation: the mind and the body; reason and feelings' (Evans 1997: 242). In the work 'Narratives of Dis-Ease' Spence, in collaboration with Dr. Tim Sheard, produced a set of five colour photographic portraits, 'Excised', 'Expunged', 'Expected', 'Exiled' and 'Included?'. It is only in the last one that we see her face, the person not as patient, crying as she clutches a teddy bear to her naked body. Each image deals with different aspects of her life living with breast cancer, her fears, expectations and desires. In the picture 'Exiled', Spence opens the medical gown she is wearing to reveal a naked torso, with the word MONSTER written large across her chest. It is also possible to make out that she is wearing a *Phantom of the Opera* mask. Spence makes a spectacle of herself; by playing up to the notion of the grotesque and the label of 'freak', she challenges our definition of the natural order of things.

Sociologist Simon Williams (1998), in a critique of Leder's absent body theory, uses Bakhtin's ideas of the carnivalesque to explore the freak show, its parades and parodies, as a useful way to challenge the normal modes of bodily disappearance it invites. Rather than behave properly it actually celebrates the body and all its versions and differences. Margrit Shildrick also confirms this opinion when she claims 'monsters clearly cannot exist apart from 'normal' bodies, but at the same time they are excessive to the binary, uncontained by any fixed category of exclusion...they refuse to stay in place: they change shape, they combine elements which should remain separate'. She concludes: 'Monsters signify, then, not the oppositional other safely fenced off within its own boundaries, but the otherness of possible worlds, or possible versions of ourselves, not yet realised' (Shildrick 1996: 8).

Simon was aware of the 'freaky' nature of his body, this was after all his performance for the camera, a non-conformist body that is both disruptive and transgressive. As a member of various direct action groups such as Act-Up and Outrage! Simon strongly believed in 'the personal is political', rather than just the body re-membered as alien; this was the apprehension of

Figure 11.3 Exiled (from the 'Narratives of Dis-Ease' series) 1990, © Terry Bennett, Jo Spence Memorial Archive.

a lived experience and a desire to make that experience visible to himself and to society. A medical model of this split, between the body and the self, would tell us that if we heal it then the body would be able to return to the 'normal' productive world (McGrath 1984: 15), the emphasis being on the productive as in terms of being healthy and able to reproduce. To recover signifies an act of covering, of hiding what went before. However, in a time of regular health scares, including HIV and AIDS, does the body ever totally disappear?

Bodies of Resistance

From the evidence of numerous art works and exhibitions still being produced about AIDS, the body is still very much an issue of concern, although perhaps not as high a profile as it used to be since AIDS has been devalued as a threat to society in the West. However one such exhibition, 'Bodies of Resistance' (2000), offers insights into how AIDS has shaped visual culture and how it has influenced artistic representations of the body. Julia Bryan-Wilson and Barbara Hunt, writing in the catalogue to the exhibition, tell us that 'the very terms of the body are currently being drastically revised by AIDS and HIV [...] the effect of the AIDS pandemic is shifting the discourses of the body in innumerable and often intangible ways' (2000: 10).

Examples of this can be seen in the recent photographs of various artists working in Britain today who, with different intentions, explore the in/visibility of the body as a central theme to their work. In the photographs of Dominic Harris, like Simon a gay man with AIDS but unwilling to document his body in the same way, a metaphor is created for the body by replacing it with a receptacle, in this case a decorative garden flower container known as a planter. The drugs, walking stick, medical paraphernalia, placed in the planter, are the constituents of being. As Harris puts it himself, 'I watched my body deteriorate to a point where I barely recognised it. A simple vessel might as well replace me' (Harris 1998: 3). Through the process of observation he objectifies himself. This objectification could be read as both a reaction to the continuous consultations and exploration by the medical profession, and as a result of the cultural climate in the gay world. Harris openly admits his nervousness about going to a gay bar with a walking stick, which projects the representation of a diseased body, not the healthy, good, beautiful body that it should be, i.e. recessive rather than ecstatic. The over compensation within the gay community to appear not to be 'diseased', to distance itself from the historical medical classification as pathological, has created its own fantasy of the 'normal'. The artists Barrett-Forster have commented on how anyone surveying

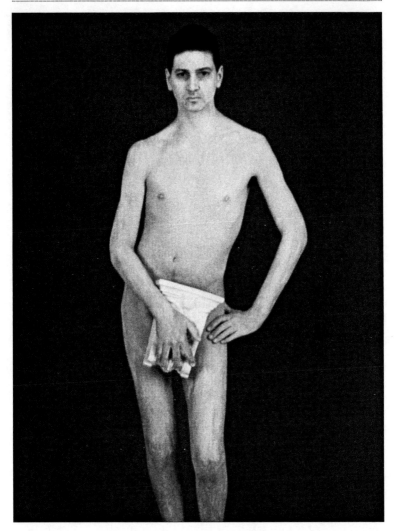

Figure 11.4 Self Portrait No. 1, 1997 © Dominic Harris.

HIV-related visual material in the United Kingdom gay / HIV media might be forgiven for thinking that HIV gives you a gorgeous body. In the United Kingdom at least the reaction against early tabloid newspaper photographs of emaciated People With AIDS (PWAs), has led to a powerful taboo against any images of symptoms, wasting, or indeed even of cheerful symptomatic people.[8]

When Harris was extremely ill he wrote that thoughts of sex were long in the past and it might be a subconscious reaction to replace his sexual organs with another body as in 'Self Portrait No.1'. The sexual organs connect the exterior and interior worlds, their absence engenders beings unable to construct themselves as subjects. What is the real body if not the sexual body? Harris creates a complex contradiction in this photograph by combining the planter and himself. While it is possible to think of the receptacle in the dictionary definition of, 'the part of lower plants that bears the reproductive organs or spores',[9] the receptacle now hides or even contains his genitalia. It is a metaphor for only one thing now, his sexual organs. (Although his physical body is represented in the image it is absent from the real body – the sexual organs.) In the image of Simon, although his genitalia are clearly visible the disfigurement or their grotesque nature appears to make them and therefore Simon himself invalid as a subject. While Canogar writes that the castration of the subjects depicted in Aziz and Cucher's work is by digital manipulation his comment that 'it is the incomprehensibility of sex that makes the genitals appear as monstrous protuberances and excrescences' (Canogar 1999: 262) could equally apply to Simon. Although not explicitly about AIDS, the fact that Cucher is also HIV positive could be said to inflect his collaborative work. He has spoken in the same way as Harris about his near-disappearing body, but how now, due to drugs developed out of research in bio-engineering, it is restored if not cured:

> In the mid to late 80's in relation to AIDS, the abjection of the body was its 'truth'; one couldn't understand the body any other way because all we knew was illness and death. Now the reality of living with AIDS as an active body with a future is my reality.[10]

The photographer Sunil Gupta has constantly documented his appearance and his body through the years, developing an allegorical language of his own as a way of dealing with living in 'other' culture double or treble. His unassuming photographs talk deeply about the nature of photography. In the 'Exile' series Gupta sets up images of other Asian gay men in various outdoor locations in India: not behind closed doors shut away but moving in and out of shared spaces. He comments 'I wanted to show what they look like. I wanted to show that they look like anybody else, i.e., 'normal', which is what appears to be their most frightening aspect...their invisibility is both their strength and weakness' (Gupta 1999: 1). The normal is here again associated with the invisible or absence, to

Figure 11.5 Lodhi Gardens (from the 'Exiles' series), 1987/99
© Sunil Gupta.

be exiled in one's own country. In the photographic diptychs,
'From Here to Eternity', a comment on still living, Gupta contrasts a series of self-portraits with exteriors of well known
South London gay clubs. Portraits, such as the blood test shot
at his local clinic, which reveal the routine of medical surveil-
lance as a reminder of the constant checking of the diseased
body; the viewer participates in observing the observation
process. This is a ritual that acknowledges, literally, the fluidity of the body and his own ambivalent position as voyeuristic
spectator and subject of disease. Other portraits find him pho-
tographing himself in a hotel-room mirror or documenting
his body at home with his English Christmas decorations.
These deceptively simply constructed images reveal an awareness of how our body is always responded to in a particu-
larised fashion, with different identities becoming more
pronounced to the viewer at different times and in different

Figure 11.6 Chicago Hoist (from the 'From Here to Eternity' series) 1999 © Sunil Gupta.

spaces. Images of closed exteriors of sex clubs are juxtaposed against the portraits, creating an absence as they appear to exclude Gupta. Is it because he is Asian, old or HIV positive? On writing about Spence, Jessica Evans, a visual culture critic, makes a distinction, adapted from de Certeau's *The Practice of Everyday Life*, between 'place', independent from individuals who may occupy it and 'space', somewhere one makes use of. This could equally apply to some of the hospital images by Harris and Gupta as to Spence. Evans writes

> In her 'self-documentary' pictures, made as patient when in hospital diagnosed with breast cancer, Spence challenges not just the infantillisation of being a subject-patient but also puts the subject back into the body of the patient. Taking pictures is to enter into immediate performed relationships with a particular setting, to stage an interaction with an environment which alters during the process. The hospital system is no longer depersonalised and reified as an abstract system, comparing and classifying bodies, it has been brought into consciousness as material, having effects on this person, now (Evans 1997: 241).

The duo Barrett-Forster deploy the ambiguity of photography to address the ambivalence of HIV and AIDS. They deal with a floating apprehension of the body by constructing layers of the figure revealing different details, building the image up as their repetitive motions are captured on film, reminiscent of a Francis Bacon painting, with lush colours that form streaks as the body appears and disappears into the

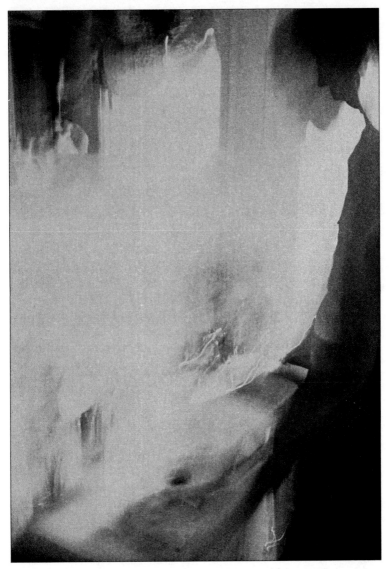

Figure 11.7 Study for Figure at Washbasin, 1994 © Barrett-Forster.

background. While their models conform to the stabilising forces within the gay community since the advent of AIDS that saw an increased visibility of bodies which were firm, hard, muscular, healthy, sexy and erotic, these idealised bodies, however, do not deny the 'mess of all our bodies', they display signs of disintegration and disappearance. 'Study for Figure at Washbasin' of a friend who has since passed on 'gives the tragic impression of a figure literally wasting away to nothing' (Dent 1999: 48). The photographic technique employed gives a ghostly appearance as white light pours in and the figure is lost amongst a blurring of form, light and colour. Emily Apter (1993), who refers to Hervé Guibert's book *Ghost Image* (1982), claims that there is more than a physical transmission of disease, with ghost-like histories that make their presence felt in those left behind. It is an illusionary perception, blurring boundaries between the body and the self, informed not just by the physical presence of the body but by the creation of another layer dependent on fantasy. In any photograph, but perhaps more so here in these ghost-like images, there is always room for our own interpretation, reading or fantasy. Earlier I quoted Watney to support the principal that the same picture of the same body can speak on behalf of its race, class or physiological condition, depending on who interprets it. He explains that, unlike ordinary sight, photography splits up our visual experience of the world. By doing so it concentrates meanings, an intensity of codes, into discrete moments of our lived experience and 'we are obliged to "fill in", by way of fantasy, an enormous amount of projective contextualisation in order to make sense of them' (Watney 1987: 4). Even when a body is absent it is not absent; the potential is there for it still to interrupt our lives.

Conclusion

It is worth making reference to Leder's interpretation of the corporeal because it helps to put into context how the body has previously been represented. He refers to German terms, traditionally used in phenomenological accounts of the body, of 'Körper' and 'Leib'. According to Leder (1990: 5), since the time of Descartes people have interpreted the body as 'Körper' rather than 'Leib', which has resulted in a rationalisation that views the physical body only as an object to be classified like any other. Leder (1990: 6) equates a living body with an embodied self that lives and breathes, perceives and acts, speaks and reasons. Unfortunately it is the 'Körper' interpretation that has been viewed as the norm as it lends itself to the demarcating categories of identity (Overboe 1999: 18). It is those who have set themselves up as the norm, as James

Overboe (1999: 18) writing about society and disability has pointed out, that have been able to preserve and defend their superior position because their normalised embodiment and sensibility sets not only the parameters of 'what the problem is', but also the limits of the discussion and the type of communication required to take part in the dialogue. Those outside the 'norm' become observed, written about, incarcerated, operated on and generally have their lived experience reduced to a classification or 'Körper' reading which demands that the 'normal' take some sort of action that implicitly or explicitly controls their lives. However those perceived as 'abnormal' will travel along different trajectories which are experienced and lived differently and are in constant flux between levels of 'normality', experience and visibility. It is for these reasons that the supposed universality of the 'abnormal', as a socially and materially created construct, is overstated in theories which seek to essentialise and dichotomise difference. The problem encountered from Leder's perspective is that it is the body's own tendency toward self-concealment that allows for the possibility of its neglect or deprecation. If the body is only to come to our attention at times of dysfunction there is the potential for it to only be seen as 'Other' and collude with the idea of mind/body split. The images of bodies as monstrous, both through crisis and celebration, interrupt the spectator's comfortable absence from conscious perception and control. Recovery from this position does not indicate a return to the 'normal', to a previous self, but an acquisition of knowledge of human corporeality that is more whole than before. What I have tried to suggest here, as in my own photographic practice, is that to understand disease as something that is not outside of oneself, that is not 'Other', we need to rethink the notion of 'abnormal' as exiled from normality.

Notes

1. I should like to thank David Company for his comments and encouragement in the preparation of this paper.
2. See Tagg, J. (1984) *The Burden of Representation*, London and Basingstoke: Macmillan, Green, D. (1985) 'On Foucault: Disciplinary Power and Photography', *Camerawork*, no. 32, Sekula, A. (1986) 'The Body and the Archive', *October*, vol. 39, Evans, J. (1988) 'The Iron Cage of Visibility', *Ten 8*, no. 29, Marshall, S. (1990), 'Picturing Deviancy' and R. McGrath, 'Dangerous Liaisons: Health, Disease and Representation', in Boffin, T. and S. Gupta (eds), *Ecstatic Antibodies: Resisting the AIDS Mythology*,

London: Rivers Oram Press, Cartwright, L. (1995) *Screening the Body: Tracing Medicine's Visual Culture*, Minneapolis: University of Minnesota Press, Roberts, R. (1997), *In Visible Light: Photography and Classification in Art, Science and the Everyday*, Oxford: Museum of Modern Art.

3. The term 'sinthome' is borrowed from Jacques Lacan who used it to indicate his move from a linguistic conception of the symptom towards a view of it as pure *jouissance* which cannot be interpreted.

4. *The Guardian*, 27 September 1997 and 17 October 1998, *The Times*, 27 September 1997, *Amateur Photographer*, 17 October 1997 and 25 October 1997, *British Journal of Photography*, 8 October 1997 and 15 October 1997, Chris Townsend, *Vile bodies: Photography and the Crisis of Looking*, Prestel, 1998, Gabriele Griffin, *Representations of HIV and AIDS: Visibility Blue/s*, Manchester University Press, 2000, Radio Four, Kaleidoscope 'End of Year Review', December 1997, GLR 94.9, Lavender Lounge, October 1997, Yorkshire Television, 'What a Picture', 15 December 1998.

5. *The Times*, 27 September 1997.

6. *Amateur Photographer*, 25 October 1997.

7. In particular see the work of Francis Galton or Cesare Lombroso in Martin Kemp and Marina Wallace, *Spectacular Bodies*, Hayward Gallery London, 2000.

8. This information was provided by e-mail correspondence between myself and the artists in October 2000.

9. Collins English Dictionary: Millennium Edition 1999.

10. Quoted in Bryan-Wilson, Julia and Barbara Hunt, *Bodies of Resistance*, New York: Visual AIDS, 2000, 21.

References

Apter, E. (1993) 'Fantom Images: Hervé Guibert and the Writing of "sida" in France', in Murphy, T. and S. Poirer (eds), *Writing AIDS*, New York: Columbia University Press.

Bryan-Wilson, J. and B. Hunt (2000) *Bodies of Resistance*, New York: Visual AIDS.

Canogar, D. (1999) 'The Obscenity of the Surface', *Espacio uno II*, Spain: Museo Nacional Centro de Arte Reina Sofia.

Corker, M. (1999) 'Disability' – The Unwelcome Ghost at the Banquet... and the Conspiracy of Normality', *Body and Society*, 5(4).

Dent, N. (1998) 'Memories', *Blue*, 21.

Douglas, M. (1995) *Purity and Danger*, London: Routledge.

Evans, J. (1997) 'An Affront to Taste? The Disturbances of Jo Spence', in Evans, J. (ed.), *The Camerawork Essays*, London: Rivers Oram Press.

Foster, H. (1996) 'Obscene, Abject, Trauma', *October*, 78.

Gilman, S. (1995) *Health and Illness: Images of Difference*, London: Reaktion.

Gupta, S. (1999) *Exiles*, London: Gupta.

Harris, D. (1998) *Index of Optimism*, London: Harris.

Kristeva, J. (1982) *Powers of Horror*, New York: Columbia University Press.

Leder, D. (1990) *The Absent Body*, Chicago: University of Chicago Press.

McGrath, R. (1984) 'Medical Police', *Ten 8*, 14.

McGrath, R. (1995) 'Geographies of the Body and the Histories of Photography', *Camera Austria International*, 51/52.

Overboe, J. (1999) 'Difference in Itself: Validating Disabled People's Lived Experience', *Body and Society*, 5(4).

Shildrick, M. (1996) 'Posthumanism and the Monstrous Body', *Body and Society*, 2(1).

Watney, S. (1987) 'The Image of the Body', *Figures*, Cambridge: Cambridge Darkroom.

Williams, S. (1998) 'Bodily Dys-Order: Desire, Excess and the Transgression of Corporeal Boundaries', *Body and Society*, 4(2).

Notes on Contributors

Feroza Basu is a graduate of Oxford University. She is currently involved in postgraduate research at the University of Liverpool, as part of an AHRB-sponsored project entitled 'New Approaches toTwentieth Century Travel Literature in French'. Her individual research within this project concerns recent innovations in definitions of travel, and the intersection of travel writing, travel theories and touristic practices.

Wendy Everett is Senior Lecturer in French and Film at the University of Bath. Her principal research interests are in European cinema, and her publications in this field include *European Identity in Cinema* (Intellect, 1996), and *The Seeing Century: Film, Vision, and Identity* (Rodopi, 2000), as well as numerous journal articles and book chapters, including 'Double Vision: Narcissus and the Silver Screen' in *Echoes of Narcissus* for Berghahn. She has recently completed a book on the British director Terence Davies, to be published by Manchester University Press (2004).

Gabriele Griffin is Professor of Gender Studies at the University of Hull. Her research focuses on women's cultural production and issues of gender. She is coordinator of an EU-funded research project on 'Women's Studies Training and Women's Employment in Europe'; and co-founding editor of Feminist Theory (Sage). She has co-edited (with Rosi Braidotti) *Thinking Differently: A Reader in European Women's Studies* (ZED Books, 2002), and has written the *Who's Who in Lesbian and Gay Writing* (Routledge, 2002). Her current research centres on

Contemporary Black Women Playwrights in Britain (Cambridge University Press, 2003).

Chris Horrocks is Senior Lecturer in Art History at the Faculty of Art, Design and Music, Kingston University. His publications include *Postmodern Encounters: Marshall McLuhan and Virtuality* and *Introducing Baudrillard* (Icon Books). His essays for Berghahn include a critique of feminist approaches to Duchamp, in the book *Secret Spaces, Forbidden Places*. He is currently researching a book on art, philosophy and technology.

Catherine Lupton is Senior Lecturer in Film Studies at the University of Surrey Roehampton. She is currently writing a book on the work of Chris Marker, to be published by Reaktion, and has contributed articles to the Wallflower *Directory of Contemporary European Directors* (forthcoming 2003) and the *Encyclopedia of Documentary* (forthcoming 2003).

Richard Sawdon Smith is Senior Lecturer in Photography at The Surrey Institute of Art and Design, University College. His photographs are published in a number of books including; *Fully Exposed: The Male Nude in Photography* (1990), Emmanuel Cooper; *Vile Bodies: Photography and the Crisis of Looking* (1998), Chris Townsend and *Representations of HIV and AIDS: Visibility Blue/s* (2000), Gabriele Griffin. His work has been exhibited widely including Galerie Godante (1992), 'solo show', Kobe, Japan; Belem Cultural Centre (1998), Expo'98 – A Stroll Through the Century', Lisbon, Portugal; La Calcografia Nacional (1999), 'A Plena Luz' (Into the Light), Madrid, Spain; National Portrait Gallery (1997), 'John Kobal Photographic Portrait Award', London, England & The Scottish National Portrait Gallery (1998), Edinburgh, Scotland.

Deborah Schultz is a Research Fellow at the University of Sussex. She completed her doctorate in history of art at the University of Oxford in 1998 on 'Marcel Broodthaers: Strategy and Dialogue'. Since 1998 she has been a Visiting Lecturer at Central St Martin's School of Art & Design. Recent publications include *On the Prevalence of Maps in Contemporary Art*, Henry Moore Institute, 2001 and 'Us and them, this and that, here and there, now and then: collecting, classifying, creating', co-authored with Martin Kemp, in *Strange and Charmed. Science and the Contemporary Visual Arts*, Siân Ede (ed.), Calouste

Gulbenkian Foundation, London, 2000. She is a regular contributor to *Art Monthly*.

Lieve Spaas is Research Professor of Arts and Culture at Kingston University. She is the author of various articles and books on film and eighteenth century anthropological thought. Her most recent books are *The Francophone Film: a struggle for identity* (Manchester University Press, 2000), and *Le Cinéma nous parle: stratégies narratives du film* (Debrecen University Press, Hungary, 2000). She is currently working on *Remembering the Congo*, an interdisciplinary project that explores how the Congo has been represented and remembered through different media.

Christine Sprengler is Assistant Professor in the Visual Arts Department, University of Western Ontario. Her doctoral dissertation examines nostalgia and cultural memory in contemporary British cinema. She has lectured in Cultural Studies and Art and Visual Theory Departments at the University of East London, and has published work in Film and History.

Carrie Tarr is a Research Fellow at Kingston University. She has published widely on gender and ethnicity in French cinema. Her recent publications include *Diane Kurys* (Manchester University Press, 1999), *Women, Immigration and Identities in France* (co-edited with Jane Freeman, Berg, 2000), and *Cinema and the Second Sex: Women's Filmmaking in France in the 1980s and 1990s* (with Brigitte Rollet, Continuum, 2001).

Peter Wagstaff is Senior Lecturer in French at The University of Bath. His research interests are chiefly in autobiography, from the eighteenth century to the present, and questions of identity in a cross-national context. He is currently editing a book on *Mapping Identities in Modern Europe: an Examination of Transnational Culture*, and contributing a chapter on regional identities in *Cultures and Identities in Europe* (Berghahn). Other recent and forthcoming publications include articles for the Fitzroy Dearborn *Encyclopedia of Life Writing* and the ABC-CLIO *Encyclopedia of the French Atlantic*.

SELECT BIBLIOGRAPHY

Arenas, R. (1993) *Before Night Falls: A Memoir*, translated by
  D. M. Koch, London: Penguin.
Armes, R. (1985) *French Cinema*, London: Secker and Warburg.
Aubenas, J. (1995) *Catalogue des films de Chantal Akerman*
  (R. Dehaye, ed.), Bruxelles: Commissariat Général aux
  Relations Internationales de la Communauté Française de
  Belgique.
Barthes, R. (1980) *La Chambre claire*, Paris: *Cahiers du Cinéma*,
  Gallimard, Seuil. English translation by Richard Howard (1982)
  Camera Lucida, London: Jonathan Cape.
Barthes, R. (1993) *Oeuvres complètes*, vol. 1, Paris: Editions du Seuil.
Bartkowski, Frances (1995) *Travellers, Immigrants, Inmates: Essays in
  Estrangement*, Minneapolis, MN: University of Minnesota Press.
Baudrillard, J. (1986) *Amérique*, Paris: Bernard Gasset. English
  translation by C. Turner (1988) *America*, London: Verso.
Baudrillard, J. (1996) *The Perfect Crime*, London and New York: Verso.
Bauman, Z. (1993) *Postmodern Ethics*, Oxford: Blackwell.
Bell, D. and G. Valentine (eds) (1995) *Mapping Desire: geographies of
  sexualities*, London: Routledge.
Bellos, D. (1993) *Georges Perec: A Life in Words*, London: Harvill.
Biro, M. (1998) *Anselm Kiefer and the Philosophy of Martin Heidegger*,
  Cambridge and New York: Cambridge University Press.
Bockris, V. (1998) *The Life and Death of Andy Warhol*, London: Fourth
  Estate Limited.
Bohm-Duchen, M. (1987) *Arnold Daghani*, London: Diptych.
Bohm-Duchen, M. (ed.) (1995) *After Auschwitz: Responses to the
  Holocaust in Contemporary Art*, Sunderland and London: Northern
  Centre for Contemporary Art, in association with Lund
  Humphries.
Bordo, S. (1993) *Unbearable Weight: Feminism, Western Culture, and
  the Body*, Berkeley: University of California Press.

Bourdieu, P. (1977) *Outline of a Theory of Practice*, Cambridge: Cambridge University Press.

Bruzzi, S. (2000) *New Documentary: A Critical Introduction*, London: Routledge.

Bryan-Wilson, J. and B. Hunt (2000) *Bodies of Resistance*, New York: Visual AIDS.

Butler, J. (1993) *Bodies that Matter: On The Discursive Limits of 'Sex'*, London and New York: Routledge.

Case, S.-E., P. Brett, and S. Leigh Foster (eds) (1995) *Cruising the Performative*, Bloomington: Indiana University Press.

Chirimuuta, R.C. and R. J. Chirimuuta (1987) *Aids, Africa and Racism*, Stanhope, Derbyshire: Chirimuuta.

Cohan, S. and I. R. Hark (1997) *The Road Movie Book*, London and New York: Routledge.

Corrigan, T. (1991) *A Cinema Without Walls: Movies and Culture after Vietnam*, New Brunswick, New Jersey: Rutgers University Press.

Crimp, D. with A. Rolston (1990) *AIDSDEMOGRAPHICS*, Seattle: Bay Press.

Crone, R. (1970) *Andy Warhol*, New York: Praeger.

Crone, R. and W. Wiegand (1972) *Die revolutionäre Ästhetik Andy Warhols*, Darmstadt: Melzer Verlag.

Daghani, Arnold (1961) *The Grave is in the Cherry Orchard*, London: Adam.

Deleuze, G. (1986) *Cinema 1: the Movement-Image*, London: Athlone.

Dick, E., A. Noble and D. Petrie (eds) (1993) *Bill Douglas: A Lanternist's Account*, London: British Film Institute.

Douglas, M. (1995) *Purity and Danger*, London: Routledge.

Doyle, J., J. Flatley, and J. E. Muñoz (eds) (1996) *Pop Out: Queer Warhol*, Durham and London: Duke University Press.

Evans, J. (ed.) (1997) *The Camerawork Essays*, London: Rivers Oram Press.

Falk, P. (1994) *The Consuming Body*, London: Sage.

Feinberg, L. (1993) *Stone Butch Blues*, New York: Firebrand Books.

Felstiner, J. (1995) *Paul Celan: Poet, Survivor, Jew*, New Haven and London: Yale University Press.

Ferguson, M. (1983) *Forever Feminine: Women's Magazines and the Cult of Femininity*, London: Heinemann Educational Books.

Fonseca, I. (1996) *Bury Me Standing: The Gypsies and their Journey*, New York: Vintage.

Gilman, S. (1995) *Health and Illness*, London: Reaktion.

Griffin, G. (2000) *Representations of HIV and AIDS: Visibility Blue/s*, Manchester: Manchester University Press.

Gupta, S. (1999) *Exiles*, London: Gupta.

Hall, M. (1996) *Leaving Home. A conducted tour of twentieth-century music with Simon Rattle*, London: Faber and Faber.

Harris, D. (1998) *Index of Optimism*, London: Harris.

Harvey, D. (1989) *The Condition of Postmodernity*, Cambridge, Mass. and Oxford: Blackwell.

Hayward, S. (1996) *Key concepts in cinema studies*, London and New York: Routledge.

Hearn, G. (1992) *Men in the Public Eye: The Construction and Deconstruction of Public Men and Public Patriarchies*, London: Routledge.

Heritage, J. (1984) *Garfinkel and Ethnomethodology*, Cambridge: Polity.

Hobsbawm, E. and T. Ranger (eds) (2000) *The Invention of Tradition*, Cambridge: Cambridge University Press.

Huyssen, A. (1995) *Twilight Memories: Marking Time in a Culture of Amnesia*, London: Routledge.

Jones, C. A. (1996) *Machine in the Studio: Constructing the Postwar American Artist*, Chicago and London: University of Chicago Press.

Kristeva, J. (1982) *Powers of Horror: An Essay on Abjection*, New York: Columbia University Press.

Kristeva, J. (1991) *Strangers to Ourselves*, London: Harvester Wheatsheaf.

Kuspit, D. (1996) *Idiosyncratic Identities: Artists at the End of the Avant-Garde*, Cambridge: Cambridge University Press.

LaCapra, D. (1985) *History and Criticism*, London: Cornell University Press.

Landor, G. and C. Robson (eds) (2000) *Balkan Plots: Plays from Central and Eastern Europe*, London: Aurora Metro Press.

Langer, L. L. (1991) *Holocaust Testimonies: The Ruins of Memory*, New Haven and London: Yale University Press.

Leder, D. (1990) *The Absent Body*, Chicago: University of Chicago Press.

Levi, P. (2000) *If This is a man. The Truce*, London: Everyman.

Lingus, A. (1994) *Foreign Bodies*, London: Routledge.

Longhurst, R. (2001) *Bodies: exploring fluid boundaries*, London and New York: Routledge.

Margulies, I. (1996) *Nothing Happens: Chantal Akerman's Hyperrealist Everyday*, Durham and London: Duke University Press.

Marker, C. (1961) *Commentaires*, Paris: Editions du Seuil.

McDonald, K. and M. Cousins (eds) (1996) *Imagining Reality: The Faber Book of Documentary*, London: Faber and Faber.

Menchú, R. (1984) *I, Rigoberta Menchú: An Indian Woman in Guatemala*, London: Verso.

Monk, C. and A. Sargeant (eds) (2002) *British Historical Cinema*, London: Routledge.

Morris, J. (1974) *Conundrum: An Extraordinary Narrative of Transsexualism*, London: Henry Holt.

Moure, G. (1996) *Christian Boltanski: Advent and Other Times*, Barcelona: Editions Polígrafa and Santiago de Compostela, Centro Galego de Arte Contemporánea.

Murphy, T. and S. Poirer (eds) (1993) *Writing AIDS*, New York: Columbia University Press.

Naficy, H. (ed.) (1999) *Home, Exile, Homeland: Film, Media and the Politics of Place*, London and New York: Routledge/American Film Institute Film Readers.

Orlan (1996) *Ceci est mon corps... ceci est mon logiciel...*, London: Black Dog Publishing.

Perec, G. (1969) *La Disparition*, Paris, Gallimard. English translation by G. Adair (1996) *A Void*, London, Harvill.

Perec, G. (1975) *W ou le souvenir d'enfance*, Paris: Denoël. English translation by D. Bellos (1989) *W or the Memory of Childhood*, London, Harvill.

Phelan, P. (1997) *Mourning Sex: Performing Public Memories*, London: Routledge.

Piper, A. (1996) *Out of Order, Out of Sight Vol. 1: Selected Writings in Meta-Art 1968–1992*, Cambridge, Mass.: MIT Press.

Roberts, J. (1998) *The art of interruption: Realism, photography and the everyday*, Manchester and New York: Manchester University Press.

Robinson, M. (ed.) (1994) *Altogether Elsewhere: Writers on Exile*, New York: Harcourt Brace.

Rosenstone, R. (1995) *Visions of the Past: The Challenge of Film to Our Idea of History*, Cambridge MA and London: Harvard University Press.

Russell, C. (1999) *Experimental Ethnography*, Durham NC: Duke University Press, 1999.

Saïd, E. W. (2001) *Reflections on Exile and Other Literary and Cultural Essays*, London: Granta Books.

Samuel, R. (1994) *Theatres of Memory*, London: Verso.

Silverman, K. (1996) *The Threshold of the Visible World*, New York and London: Routledge.

Sorlin, P. (1991) *European Cinemas, European Societies 1939–1990*, London and New York: Routledge.

Steedman, C. (1986) *Landscape for a Good Woman*, London: Virago.

Stoll, D. (1999) *Rigoberta Menchú and the Story of All Poor Guatemalans*, Boulder, Colorado: Westview Press.

Stone, A. R. (1996) *The War of Desire and Technology at the Close of the Mechanical Age*, Cambridge, MA: MIT Press.

Trachtenberg, A. (ed.) (1980) *Classic Essays on Photography*, New Haven, Connecticut: Leete's Island Books.

Urbain J-D. (1998) *Secrets de voyage: Menteurs, imposteurs et autres voyageurs invisibles*, Paris: Essais Payot.

Virilio, P. (1989) *Esthétique de la disparition*, Paris: Editions Galilée. English translation by Philip Beitchman (1991) *The Aesthetics of Disappearance*, New York: Autonomedia.

Warhol, A. (1977) *The Philosophy of Andy Warhol (From A to B and Back Again)*, San Diego, New York and London: Harvest.

Watney, S. (1994) *Practices of Freedom: Selected Writings on HIV/AIDS*, London: Rivers Oram Press.

White, H. (1973) *Metahistory: The Historical Imagination in Nineteenth-Century Europe*, London: The Johns Hopkins University Press.

SELECT FILMOGRAPHY

Akerman, C., *Blow Up my Town* [*Saute ma ville*] (Belgium,1968)
Hôtel Monterey (USA/Belgium,1972)
Jeanne Dielman, 23 Quai du Commerce, 1080 Bruxelles
(Belgium/France, 1975)
News from Home (France/West Germany/Belgium, 1976)
Les Rendez-vous d'Anna (France/Germany/Belgium, 1978)
Histoires d'Amérique (Belgium/France,1989)
From the East [*D'Est*] (Belgium/France/Portugal,1993).
Angelopoulos, T., *The Suspended Step of the Stork* [*To Meteoro vima tou pelargou*] (France/Greece/Italy/Switzerland, 1991)
Ulysses' Gaze [*To Vlemma tou Odyssea*] (Greece/France/Italy, 1995)
Eternity and a Day [*Mia aiwniothta kai mia mera*]
(France/Italy/Greece, 1998)
Douglas, B., *Trilogy: My Childhood* (United Kingdom, 1972), *My Ain Folk* (United Kingdom, 1973), *My Way Home* (United Kingdom, 1978)
Fridriksson, F. T., *Cold Fever* [Á köldum klaka] (United States/Japan/Iceland, 1994)
Gatlif, T., *Les Princes* (France, 1983)
Mondo (France, 1996)
The Crazy Stranger [*Gadjo dilo*] (France/Romania, 1998)
I Come [*Vengo*] (France/Germany/Spain/Japan, 2000)
Hitchcock, A., *Vertigo* (United States, 1958)
Kaurismäki, A., *Leningrad Cowboys Go America* (Finland, 1989)
Koller, X., *Journey of Hope* [*Reise der Hoffnung*] (Turkey/Switzerland, 1990)
Lichtefeld, P., *Trains 'N' Roses* [*Zugvögel... einmal nach Inari*] (Germany/Finland, 1997)
Marker, C., *A Sunday in Peking* [*Dimanche à Pékin*] (France, 1955)
Letter from Siberia [*Lettre de Sibérie*] (France, 1958)

The Pier [*La Jetée*] (France, 1962)

If I Had Four Camels [*Si j'avais quatre dromedaires*] (France/West Germany, 1966)

Sunless [*Sans Soleil*] (France, 1982)

Moretti, N., *Dear Diary* [*Caro diario*] (Italy, 1994)

Pawlikowski, P., *Last Resort* (United Kingdom, 2001)

Perec, G. and R. Bober, *Récits d'Ellis Island: histoires d'errance et d'espoir* (France, 1980)

Truffaut, F., *The 400 Blows* [*Les 400 Coups*] (France, 1959)

Wenders, W., *Alice in the Cities* [*Alice in den Städten*] (West Germany, 1974)

Kings of the Road [*Im Lauf der Zeit*] (West Germany, 1975)

Paris, Texas (United Kingdom /France/West Germany, 1984)

INDEX